Too Small

Why Atheists Can't Know What They Say They Know

Craig Biehl

Tulip Publishing
Lansvale, New South Wales, Australia

Most Scripture quotations are from:
New American Standard Bible (NASB) © 1960, 1977, 1995
by the Lockman Foundation. Used by permission.

Also quoted is the King James Version (KJV).

For information contact:

Tulip Publishing, PO Box 3150, Lansvale, NSW, Australia 2166

www.tulippublishing.com.au

Book design by Tulip Publishing
Cover design by Darko Bovan

PAPERBACK ISBN: 978-1-922584-11-3

DIGITAL ISBN: 978-1-922584-12-0

NATIONAL LIBRARY OF AUSTRALIA

A catalogue record for this work is available from the National Library of Australia

"This is a marvelous book. I have often thought, there must be a God: how else do you explain Bach's Passacaglia or Brahms' Requiem? Dr. Biehl's refutations of atheism are air-tight. Despite the rumors, atheism is alive and well, especially in the West. This book hits atheism head on but with a carefully laid-out counter argument. Dr. Biehl exposes hidden assumptions and gift-wrapped evidence in order to highlight a biblical alternative. Not only, as the title declares, is atheism too small, but it is actually counterproductive. This book deserves a wide reading."

Dr. William Edgar
Professor Emeritus of Apologetics
Westminster Theological Seminary, Pennsylvania, USA

"Having been involved in debating and discussing with atheists and agnostics for many years, there is one flaw in their argument which is so obvious that it is usually ignored. Not by Craig Biehl, who in this rather brilliant book points out why the grand presumption of atheism is false. The presumption that human beings have the ability to sit in judgement upon God is the great falsehood which Biehl exposes. It's not the lack of evidence that is the problem—it's a person's inability to evaluate that evidence. Biehl then goes on to deal with the main arguments against ('disproofs') the existence of God—including philosophical, moral, and 'biblical' objections. This is a short, serious, and substantial book—which I wish I had had when I first took on the new fundamentalist atheists!"

David Robertson
Author, *The Dawkin Letters*

"Great book! I really enjoyed reading it. In a clear and accessible manner Craig puts the limitations of the atheist in perspective. His excellent examples and analogies help the reader grasp his logical arguments, the fallacies in atheism, and the infinite danger of putting blind faith in their finite speculations. It is a compelling book, and I highly recommend it."

Hampton Keathley
Executive Director, Bible.Org

"In his latest book, *Too Small*, Dr. Biehl effectively dismantles the arguments of atheists by exposing the limitations and false presuppositions of those who would explain ultimate realities beyond what God has told us in Scripture. I strongly recommend this book to all believers, especially to those who are actively engaging with evangelism and missions."

Roger Kim
President, Westminster Theological College and Seminary, Cambodia

"Craig Biehl masterfully turns the table on atheists by attacking the very foundation of their belief system. Biehl doesn't get sidetracked by answering all the objections of atheists. Neither does he seek to prove God's existence based on accepting the presuppositions of atheists. Instead, Biehl pulls the rug from underneath atheists by exposing that they are in no position to claim that they know what they think they know. The fundamental problem with atheism is that it is built on blind faith. Atheism is constructed on the false assumption that man has intellectual self-autonomy. Without warrant, atheists uncritically assume they are in an authoritative position to build a rational explanation of everything from their finite, limited, and often flawed vantage point. Atheists err at the beginning of their inquiry into the truth. They stumble from the get-go by giving themselves too much authority in rejecting divine communication. Without the perfect revelation of God's self-disclose, man is left in the darkness, and the worldview he contrives will always end in absurdity. After rejecting the false assumption of atheism, Biehl explains the reasonableness of Christianity as the only consistent explanation of everything. What I love most about this book is its concise chapters. It is a beautiful book that answers some of life's most important questions. By God's grace, this will be a help to many."

Dr. Jeffrey D. Johnson,
President, Grace Bible Theological Seminary,
Arkansas, USA

Contents

Foreword for *Too Small*

Dr. Tom J. Nettles

Do atheists have the ability and knowledge to know that God doesn't exist?" Biehl asks this question in a score or more of different ways. He shows, humorously but with penetrating insight throughout, the presumptuous character of atheistic confidence in their ability to disprove God. For example, the folly of the atheists' claim to absolute knowledge that there are no absolutes is shown by the simple observation, "On a good day, we might remember where we put the car keys, but we still can't know the contents of our neighbour's basement without a look (or the neighbour telling us)." He goes through the entire house eventually, each time demonstrating our ignorance apart from empirical discovery or personal revelation. The point he makes is that true intellectual honesty calls for "a proper and heartfelt understanding of our smallness." Can any person honestly feel qualified to give such an absolutist assertion against absolutes?

Again, he asks, "How do atheists know what they claim to know? And are the assumptions behind their interpretations of scientific discoveries justified, reasonable, and consistent with the nature of reality?" By his repetition of the well-placed question—and the multiplicity of ways in which he gives a "no" answer—Biehl demonstrates that the human mind and even the most vast expanse of human knowledge is just "Too Small" to conclude that God does not exist.

The atheism he investigates is particularly "Christian atheism." No other god presents any challenge to those who feel enough intellectual robustness to disprove God. He is the infinite one; he is the singularly compelling almighty one. He is the Creator and the judge who holds men accountable for sins yet finds a way to forgive. Reduce him to nothing, and the field is clear. Disprove the existence of this God that Christians claim has revealed himself in a testable, verifiable, and yet transcendently expansive way and you have warded off the moral pressure that the God of creation, providence, redemption, and final judgement is actually there.

Biehl engages chapter by chapter the painfully ostentatiously titled book *The Impossibility of God.* Layer by layer, argument by argument, Biehl shows the futility of both the authors' arguments and their confidence. They assert their disproofs in pursuit of God's impossibility by syllogism built on the propositions of biblical revelation but omit vital aspects of the needed material for a sound major premise. "Atheists, it seems, presume God and moral standards in order to criticise and explain Him away." But our author also points out that not only is the biblical perspective subjected to radical reductionism, but their own authorities are bloated with an unwarranted expansionism. "Not only do atheists assume they can know what they can't know," Biehl observes, "they also treat their perspective and opinion as the final measure of what's possible. Claiming science and reason, they embrace irrationality and blind faith."

Though the overall impact of Biehl's interaction with the atheists is withering in its effect, he is not uncivil, disrespectful, or merely dismissive. He puts each argument in its best light but continually points out the fatal error of an assumed omniscience: "the best atheist arguments rest only on mere guesswork." He reiterates that theme throughout, not without warrant, as he demonstrates that the assertion of the disproofs fails to connect with the coherent complexity and the multifaceted simplicity of the God of biblical revelation: "They call guesswork 'reasonable' and 'scientific.' They label as 'facts' that which they cannot possibly know. And they have blind faith in their presumed ability to know the unknowable."

Always hovering over the tightness of Biehl's analyses and his untiring demonstration of their misplaced overconfidence, is an edifying reminder of the beauty and glory of the God revealed in the Bible. And why not? The grandeur of the one, true God in His triune glory should always be displayed when unbelievers seek to assault His firm reality and unsurpassable excellence. Biehl acts consistently as a believer and wants God Himself to appear when He is the subject of discussion. The pertinent biblical citations add to the impression of how impossible is the task of disproving such a God.

Each chapter is brief at between one and four pages long, except chapter 29. It is rightfully the longest for there Biehl deals with the objection that a god who is perfectly just cannot be a god who shows mercy; and a god who shows mercy cannot possibly be a god who is perfectly just. The God of the Bible, therefore, does not exist. It is this precise tension, an apparent impossibility, that Paul treats in Romans 3:21-26. This opens the door for a full presentation of the gospel. It is gripping, clear, fully submissive to divine revelation and a thorough answer to the disproof of God's existence. Buy this book; enjoy reading it; grow in grace by its energetic and affecting defence of the true God; use it for a rigorous and edifying study in a theology class or church study group.

Introduction

'When we lack the will to see things as they really are,

there is nothing so mystifying as the obvious.'

Irving Kristol

The marks of God are everywhere—and everyone sees them. From the cosmos to the quark, all things give clear, compelling, convicting, and complete evidence of God's power, genius, and goodness. In the sky, in our world, and deep in our hearts, none can escape the knowledge of God. Moreover, we know God best in Scripture, in the person and ministry of Jesus Christ. Yet many will have none of this. Atheists claim that science and reason give no signs of God. Some even say that reality makes God impossible. Either way, both view atheism as more reasonable than the faith of Christianity.

All people reason by faith in an ultimate authority, though they may differ in their object of faith. Believers trust Scripture to interpret the world and ultimate realities, while atheists trust their own perspective—apart from Scripture. Both think and use logic (more or less), and both appeal to science to support their beliefs. Thus the claim that atheists stand on reason and science while believers cling to faith is false. In the following chapters we'll see that the atheists' mantra of reason opposing unreasonable faith hides their own faith and the limits of the authority in whom they trust. Given the limits of our knowledge and the conflicting history of ideas, who can we trust to answer the deepest questions and explain ultimate realities? Can we gaze beyond the universe and our experience to explain reality without the blueprint of the God who created and sustains it all? We'll see.

As for science and scientists, opinions differ. Many see God's genius in their discoveries and believe that science and our existence would be impossible without God creating, ordering, and sustaining all things. Others see time and chance behind life and the universe. Interpretations differ according to the assumptions by which we interpret the data. For instance, a Christian sees the power and genius of God behind the beauty of a flower, while the atheist sees time and chance. The most important and ultimate questions, however, lie beyond the scope of the scientific method. God as eternal spirit and things beyond the material realm cannot be examined in a lab. And whether we assume the universe has always existed or just showed up, the scientific method has never demonstrated that random chance can design or build anything, let alone the wonders of life and the world.

The Basic Question

Many issues animate the debate between atheists and Christians. But behind all the fuss lies the basic question to be addressed in this book: Do atheists have the ability and knowledge to know that God doesn't exist? Or, can atheists know what they claim to know? A simple, obvious, and vital question—but sorely ignored.

To answer it, I'll avoid traditional proofs for God, such as Aquinas's "Five Ways." Unbelief doesn't come from a lack of data or rational proof—people are drowning in evidence. Indeed, all people know that God exists: "For since the creation of the world His invisible attributes, His eternal power and divine nature, have been clearly seen, being understood through what has been made" (Rom. 1:20). All things bear the marks of His power and genius. To deny God denies the obvious.

Since I cannot add to the evidence in and around us, I won't try to prove God's existence. Instead, I'll demonstrate how human limitations, apart from God's revelation, nullify denials of the God of Scripture. I'll describe and apply the basic principle that shows how the best atheist arguments rest on mere guesswork.

Roadmap and Guidance

In Section One, we'll examine: (1) the "grand presumption" of atheism; (2) how all people view God and the world through the tinted lens of assumptions, each coloured by one's attitude toward God; (3) why the atheist's grand presumption is neither reasonable nor scientific; (4) why biblical miracles are reasonable; (5) why Bible difficulties and mysteries are normal and reasonable; (6) the problems of "naturalism"; (7) how atheists call people to entrust their eternal destiny to their opinions; and (8) why atheists cannot possibly know that God did not create all things.

Section Two analyses specific arguments from five categories of "disproofs" presented in the book *The Impossibility of God.* According to the editors, this collection of essays contains "most of the important arguments for the impossibility of God that have been published since 1948." Quite the accomplishment, but can these "important arguments" withstand a critique of the limited perspective and abilities of the authors? Do these writers have what it takes to know what they claim to know?

The critical flaw behind every denial of God's existence is simple and easy to learn. Yet knowing how to see and apply it to diverse arguments takes practice. So I humbly ask the reader to bear with some needed repetition in this book, since the same flaw of unbelief shows itself in several types of arguments. The approach used in the following chapters highlights why the basic error of atheists makes false their most logical "proofs," thereby showing us how every denial of God remains harmless to our faith. By removing the intimidation of clever and complex arguments, we can more easily and humbly engage unbelievers with truth and love *and* grow in our faith in Christ and Scripture.

Objections to faith in Christ and Scripture lose their punch when we see the blind-faith sand on which they rest. And as we observe the many ways atheists ignore their limits—limits we all share—we'll better see God's boundless glory and our need of Him for knowledge and every good thing. God, alone, can answer ultimate questions.[1] As we proceed, may we grow in our love of God's infinite excellence as seen in creation, in Scripture, and most clearly in the person and works of Christ. And may

1. For a presentation and analysis of the worldview and apologetic implications of the infinite excellence of God's perfections, see Craig Biehl, *God the Reason* (Franklin, TN: Carpenter's Son Publishing, 2015).

we mature in our approach to unbelievers with truth, love, and grace, and in such a manner that they may know we have their best interests at heart.

Challenges to the arguments of unbelief in this work may sometimes appear strident, even harsh, but no disrespect or unkindness toward the atheist is intended. Rather, the approach exposes the absurdity of arguments built on faulty assumptions in order to encourage the faith of saints and equip them to better interact with unbelievers as they share Christ. Too often we suffer unnecessary embarrassment in the face of arguments levelled against faith in Christ and Scripture. Yet we need not apologise, cower, or be intimidated by the supposed sophistication of atheistic arguments. We hold the higher ground. How and why should become evident as we proceed.

We are nothing before God, yet He sent His Son to suffer infinite wrath on the cross to pay the full penalty for our sin. He so loved us that He bought our eternal holiness and happiness—at immense cost to Himself. May God grant atheists His priceless gift of mercy and grace through saving faith in Jesus, as He so mercifully has done for us. Now, "To the King eternal, immortal, invisible, the only God, be honour and glory forever and ever. Amen" (1 Tim. 1:17).

Section One

Chapter One

The Grand Presumption of Atheism

Besides a denial of the obvious, the crucial error of atheism involves a grand presumption behind their every claim. Put simply, they presume that limited people, by themselves, can know and explain ultimate and spiritual realities, and thus answer ultimate questions.

By this basic belief, the atheist denies the existence of God, affirms the final authority of human opinion, and denies our need for God's revelation in order to know things beyond our limited viewpoint. In short, atheists trust their opinion as the final authority and standard of truth by which they interpret all things. They reason by faith in themselves. Whether this faith is rational and justified forms the basic question to be answered in this book.

Atheists presume the ability to know, apart from Scripture, what can exist beyond the known universe, things beyond their senses and three or four dimensions. They believe this, though each of them is as a speck in deep space, a flash in time—unable to know the contents of their neighbor's garage without a look. From a scant vantage point, atheists presume to know great things beyond their limited capacity.

Despite these flaws, atheists presume the ability to know things that require knowledge of everything in the universe and beyond, including every possibility. Posing a challenge to that grand presumption is the fact of human smallness in a big universe—as well as God's position as an infinite spirit who transcends that universe. Atheists thus prefer to offer arguments without first considering their limitations. They ignore their starting assumption, since it calls into question their ability to know what they claim to know concerning ultimate realities. If, however, this starting point is faulty, all claims that rest on it fall.

A chair is only as good as its legs.

We should therefore explore the fitness of any who would explain God away. For instance, do they know everything about everything in and beyond the universe? Every possibility? Can they gain such knowledge? What do they know *for sure*? Do the boundaries of their understanding limit what can exist in and beyond the universe? Richard Dawkins, for instance, knows biology. But does he have greater access to the other side of the universe than his students? Does he know what lies beyond the three or four dimensions of his life? Not likely.

In exposing the grand presumption of atheists, we see their basic error. They call guesswork "reasonable" and "scientific." They label as "facts" that which they cannot possibly know. And they have blind faith in their presumed ability to know the unknowable.

Chapter Two

Assumptions Color All Views of God and His World

Where did this grand presumption of the atheists come from? Why do they think that they, by themselves, can know and explain ultimate and transcendent realities?

The answer highlights the basic issue of every soul.

Our View of God Colors Our View

Simply said, our view of God drives how we view everything. Do we love Him? Then we accept our smallness before His greatness. We grasp our dependence on Him for all things. We see all things as created and sustained by Him. We understand our limitations and accept Him as the source of all truth and knowledge, especially of ultimate and spiritual realities. But do we loathe Him? Then we deny our smallness before Him. We presume our independence and reject our need of Him for all things. We explain Him away and see all things as unrelated to Him. We dismiss His authority and assume it for ourselves. Thus we embrace the notion that we, by ourselves, can know and explain things beyond our experience and capacity to understand.

All people reason and interpret reality according to their love or contempt toward God. This forms the starting point of all our thinking about God and the world. From here flows a basic set of beliefs (i.e., presuppositions, assumptions, faith convictions) about God, mankind, reality, knowledge, truth, authority, and how we should live. For atheists, these basic beliefs flow from their denial of God and faith in their own ultimate authority, as follows. Concerning:

> ***God***: He doesn't exist, or if He does, He is unknowable and unimportant.
> ***Mankind***: He is uncreated and exists independent of God.
> ***Reality***: Also uncreated, independent of God, and self-sustaining.
> ***Knowledge***: Can be gained by our own effort, without God.
> ***Truth***: What we say it is, not what God says it is.
> ***Authority***: Our will and opinion, not God and Scripture.
> ***How We Should Live***: No absolute standard of right or wrong, and no punishment of evil.

From love to God and His word as the authority and object of faith, believers view God and the world according to basic beliefs contrary to those of the atheist:

> ***God***: He's the source and sustainer of all things (except sin).
> ***Mankind***: Created and dependent on God for all things.
> ***Reality***: Created, ordered, and sustained by God at all times.
> ***Knowledge***: Given by God who created and knows all things, and impossible apart from Him.
> ***Truth***: What God says it is, discovered and received by us.
> ***Authority***: God and Scripture, not personal opinion.
> ***How We Should Live***: Scripture as our standard of right and wrong, with eternal consequences for our choices.

Spectacles of Faith

From our ultimate authority and object of faith—either God or self—follow faith convictions about God, mankind, reality, knowledge, truth, authority, and how we should live. These beliefs form a tinted lens that colors how we view all things.[2] The world seen through a red lens of unbelief appears red. Obvious truth will be molded to fit the assumptions of unbelief. The world viewed through a green lens of belief appears green. Consistent

2. Colored lenses representing how our ultimate assumptions or presuppositions about God and reality "color" how we interpret all things was a favorite analogy of Cornelius Van Til. See Greg L. Bahnsen, *Van Til's Apologetic: Readings and Analysis* (Phillipsburg, NJ: P&R Publishing, 1998), 128-9.

with the assumptions of belief, creation will be rightly seen as the display of God's power, genius, and goodness. In principle, our view of all things will agree with our assumptions about God, mankind, reality, knowledge, truth, authority, and how we should live.

For example, through the colored lens of the atheist, Christ cannot be God, the Bible cannot be God's word, heaven and hell are unreal, no final authority defines or condemns sin, life and the universe formed and organized themselves, etc. Through this lens a sunset becomes an accident of time and chance instead of a display of God's genius and power. A baby becomes the product of lightning in a primal pond, the result of amino acids arranged into proteins, cell parts and the genetic code, followed by random mutations, new life forms, and survival of the fittest. And here we are.

Again, whether our reasoning begins with or without God as the creator and sustainer of all things dictates how we view all things. Deny God and everything will be viewed as unrelated to God (though not always, such as in a foxhole with bombs bursting overhead). Accept God and everything will be viewed as created, ordered, and sustained by God (though not always, given that we aren't yet perfect in glory). For the atheist, self as the final authority—as independent of God, and owing Him nothing—forms the most basic tenet of faith. For the believer, God remains the final authority, apart from whom we have nothing and to whom we owe everything. The Bible reveals His person and works in history and beyond, and serves as our guide for life and godliness. Neither atheists nor believers approach reality as neutral observers. All see the world through a set of beliefs that flow from their view of God.

No Neutrality

Nonetheless, many believe that we accept or reject God by an unbiased view of the evidence. But who is neutral toward God? To accept Him as our creator admits our debt to love, honor, and obey Him, to thank Him for every good. And as all things express His genius, power, and goodness, what lovers of independence from God will rightly interpret a world that displays their debt to submit to His authority? To see the world rightly will condemn our sinful response toward the One to whom we owe the highest love and worship. To be "neutral" or "indifferent" displays contempt. Thus, apart from God's grace in Christ, people will interpret reality in a manner that suits their desires—without God and with an assumed impunity. No wonder Jesus tells us, "He who is not with Me is against Me; and he who does not gather with Me scatters" (Matt. 12:30). No one is more polarizing than God, and no one meets with less "neutrality."

Therefore, belief *precedes* a view of the evidence and *determines* its interpretation. Our starting assumptions dictate our conclusions. And as all people interpret everything according to their most basic faith convictions about God and His world, we can see why atheists deny a designer behind the stunning design and beauty of life and the universe. We see why they view complex and universal order as a product of chaos. Having rejected God, they reject interpretations of reality that point to God, however obvious. Believers view the same world and see the evidence of God's existence and genius in everything.

So the dispute between believers and unbelievers doesn't involve "neutral" and "objective" observers who merely disagree on answers to ultimate questions. No worldview issues from "neutral" and "objective" observers. Neither does the dispute involve reason and science versus faith. All people reason by faith or trust in an ultimate authority, while both believers and unbelievers conduct and appeal to science, though they draw different conclusions from the data. Science and reason versus faith is a myth designed to discredit believers and obscure the atheists' blind faith in their own limited abilities and opinions. And what atheists call "faith" is blind faith, a leap in the dark, a notion unrelated to true Christian faith. As we'll see later, atheism rests on the blind faith they wrongly ascribe to believers.

The debate involves two opposite views of God and the world, each built on its own set of basic beliefs, and each appealing to a final authority and standard of truth in which people trust—in which they have *faith*. Atheists begin from their grand presumption, from faith in their adequacy to know and explain ultimate and spiritual realties without God. Their own perspective and opinion constitute the ultimate authority, standard of truth, and object of faith. God and Scripture constitute the same for the believer. At issue is whose object of faith can account for reality as we know it, and whose object of faith can be trusted to know and explain God, mankind, reality, knowledge, truth, authority, and how we should live?

Chapter Three

Is the Grand Presumption Reasonable?

We come to the key question concerning unbelieving and believing worldviews: Whose ultimate authority and standard of truth can be trusted to answer the deepest questions about God, man, reality, knowledge, truth, authority, and how we should live?

For the Christian, God created and sustains all things, knows all things, and thus can explain all things. And He has done so in Scripture. But in keeping with the narrow purpose of this book—to show that atheists are too small to know what they claim to know—we ask this question: Do atheists have what it takes to know and explain ultimate and spiritual realities? Do they know enough to deny God's existence? If not, how can we trust their claims about the essential nature of man, reality, knowledge, truth, authority, and how we should live?

The Need for Infinite Knowledge

To answer these and related questions, we must first ask what atheists must know in order to justify their claims. The answer, in short, is that atheists must know *everything about everything*—in the universe and beyond—including every possibility. This is what's required in order to know that God doesn't exist. It's a tall order.

Do atheists possess omniscience? If not, how can they know that God doesn't exist? Further, if they lack the infinite knowledge needed to know that, how can they know the ultimate about man's nature, reality, knowledge, truth, authority, and how we should live? It appears that the atheists' entire project begins with faith in a presumed ability to know and explain what they cannot possibly know and explain (apart from God's revelation). And if their starting presumption cannot be justified, the beliefs built on it cannot be trusted.

When atheists claim that God cannot exist because [insert claimed proof here]—we should always consider whether their abilities and vantage point are sufficient to know what they claim to know. For instance, if they deny the reality of heaven and hell, or claim that Jesus cannot be both God and man, or that He did not create all things and will not judge the world, then we ask, How do they know? If they could know that God doesn't exist, they could rightly deny what Scripture teaches. But if they lack the omniscience needed to deny God, they also lack the knowledge needed to deny that heaven and hell exist, etc. They can use logic and draw conclusions about the material world, but an infinite spirit does not belong to the material world. How can they rightly deny the reality of things that share none of the properties of the universe? They can guess and write books about their speculations, but can they know?

As we'll see later, our own perspective cannot form the standard to reject mysteries and theological puzzles because we cannot grasp or reconcile them in our mind. Our inability to know the contents of our neighbor's office or garage (without looking) makes it difficult for us to declare what exists beyond the known properties of the universe. And since God's ways are higher than our ways, "as the heavens are higher than the earth," we should expect great mysteries. The fact that our small minds cannot reconcile what Scripture says about God and His world doesn't mean those passages can't be true. But it does mean we're small compared to an infinite God.

Further, what if someone said to you, "If I cannot understand something, then it doesn't exist." Or, "God and every possible thing in and beyond the universe cannot exceed what I can fathom about it." Would you believe that person? Or would you question their sanity? Yet a great many atheists imply exactly that when they make the limits of their reason the standard of what can be true of God and His acts—or when they make the nature of earthly things the standard of what can be true of spiritual things. (More about all this later.)

Respond from Higher Ground

As we respond to unbelief, we should take care to honor God as the infinite source and sustainer of all things. He can do anything, while we depend on Him for everything, including knowledge. We need not tremble at clever or complex challenges to our faith, nor change our message to suit them. The idea that finite and fallen people form the final standard of truth and can speak with authority about ultimate reality (apart from God's revelation) not only defies reason, it destroys truth. What remains of absolute truth amid the blind-faith opinions of billions of people, none of whom are more capable of speaking about ultimate realities than anyone else? None of them can know with certainty the contents of their neighbor's dining room without a look.

If you begin with human opinion as the final standard of truth about all things in and beyond the universe, you end up only with human opinion.

Believers should therefore not abandon the high ground of God and His word by seeking to conform His explanation of Himself, of reality, and of history to guesswork. To do so dishonors God, forfeits the opportunity to expose how misplaced faith in personal opinion is behind all false views of God and the world, and blurs the human need of Christ and Scripture for truth. The atheists' trust in their opinion about things they cannot know apart from Scripture is not something we should affirm—for example, by reducing God's miracles to metaphors, or by making a global flood local, or by making the Red Sea only a few inches deep. Or worse, by placing God behind the unscientific and absurd hypothesis of evolution, thereby making death—that horrific and painful curse and enemy—God's means to advance life. This odd notion overthrows the history of redemption and makes God look more like the devil than the holy and good God of Scripture. Perhaps the fear of being called "dumb" leads us to say dumb things, while a proper grasp of the limits of those who deny God and the Bible as His Word would do much to prevent our attempts to make Scripture fit unbelief. We need not "help" God and His people by denying what God has plainly told us about Himself and the world He created.

Again, behind any view of the world stands the more basic force—love or hatred toward the God who created it. The Bible teaches that the claims of the atheist are driven by disdain toward God's authority, toward His holiness and righteous judgments, and toward His will for us. Yet for the believer, "the love of God has been poured out within our hearts through the Holy Spirit who was given to us" (Rom. 5:5). "The love of Christ controls us" (2 Cor. 5:14).

Scripture reveals that God displays His existence and attributes clearly and conspicuously in the nature of created reality (Rom. 1:18–20), in His giving us good things (Acts 14:17), and in our conscience (Rom. 2:14–15). God has opened the eyes of believers to see that "the heavens are telling of the glory of God; and their expanse is declaring the work of His hands" (Psalm 19:1). In this we rejoice—"For Thou, O LORD, hast made me glad by what Thou hast done, I will sing for joy at the works of Thy hands. How great are Thy works, O LORD!" (Psalm 92:4–5).

Chapter Four

Why Biblical Miracles Are Reasonable

Imagine your professor declaring to the class, "I know everything about everything in the universe and beyond, and about everything that could possibly exist." Imagine further that he or she was serious. Imagine even further that most people in the class agreed.

Perhaps you think that no one in their right mind would say such things. Yet many not only say it, but are honored for their brilliance in saying it, and people give their hard-earned wages to buy their books.

Who says such things? Beyond the lectern and textbooks of your local college, look no further than the countless chatrooms, videos, movies, magazines, internet articles, or your next-door neighbor. The claim is implied in every pitch that God does not exist. "Design but no Designer" goes the mantra (though many avoid the term "design," given its implications).

Again, mere mortals would need to know everything about everything in the universe and beyond, and every possibility, to know that God doesn't exist. They would need the omniscience of God to know that there is no omniscient God.

The Wonderful Behind the Wonders

Turning to God's miracles, consider this statement: "The God of the Bible cannot exist because the miracles of the Bible are impossible." But to know that biblical miracles are impossible, one must first know for certain that the God of infinite power—the God who can do *anything*—doesn't exist.

Again, to know that the God who can easily do miracles does not exist requires the impossible—knowledge of everything in and beyond the universe, including every possibility. Moreover, unbelievers appeal to uniform "laws of nature" to show that biblical miracles are impossible, and that therefore the God of the Bible doesn't exist. But such "laws" exist and operate only because God orders and upholds all things. By contrast, random chance produces nothing but chaos.

Atheists must presume God's existence to deny it. And to borrow a phrase of Jonathan Edwards, "This is not strong arguing."

Needless to say, claims that the biblical miracles are impossible in order to deny the existence of God remain unconvincing. And if the universe derives from random chance, how does random chance confirm that "natural laws" did not function differently in the past? An atheist might assume the continuous uniformity of nature, but none could know it for sure. And since order and design contradict random chance in life and the universe, the argument defeats itself by denying the worldview it seeks to affirm. Therefore, denial of the possibility of biblical miracles to deny God's existence not only ignores human limitations and the omniscience required to know that God doesn't exist, it abandons right reasoning.

Further, the notion that time and random chance have produced constant and uniform physical laws represents nothing more than a blind-faith guess—a guess contrary to logic and how everything in the universe works. It's a guess that ignores the observation, testing, and repeatability that science requires. Where, when, and how has the scientific method demonstrated such a thing? (It hasn't.) And even if one speculates that uniform and universal laws are eternal and uncaused (or *self*-caused), how does this turn speculation into science? And how does this improve the notion that universal chaos produced universal order? This merely evades the question of the how everything came to be—hardly a reasonable or scientific explanation of reality.

Again, fixed physical laws exist only because God created, organized, and upholds all things. No other account makes sense. This infers no "God of the gaps" argument—namely, that God exists despite a lack of evidence, and because nothing else makes sense. Rather, it merely says that time and chance explain nothing of the design, order, and continuous operation of anything. (How God's existence is known by everyone will be discussed in the chapter on naturalism.)

Concerning miracles, the God who designed, created, and upholds the rules can change the rules as He pleases. He can do whatever He wants, when and where He wants, for whatever reason He wants, in a manner we can't understand. Biblical miracles are therefore reasonable. When people claim to have never seen one, they merely admit their limitations. To imply that "the only things possible are things I've personally experienced" appears no more reasonable than presuming omniscience.

Finally, many of the same people who reject the miracles in Scripture believe the universe came from a blast of compressed matter the size of a golf ball or pinhead. Somehow the result formed and organized itself into everything. How then is Jonah in a whale absurd next to this? Nothing producing everything involves a far greater miracle than any act of God in the Bible. For some, it seems, anything is possible except the God of Scripture.

In fact, scientists spend millions looking for aliens and are quick to see their marks in space noise and rock formations on planets—but they see no evidence for God in the design and beauty of life and the cosmos. For them, the amazing design and order in all things—from atoms to galaxies—give evidence of *nothing*.

This irrational double standard shouldn't surprise us however. Imagined space aliens make no claims on our life or call us to repent of sin. And neither does a God defined away by time, chance, and a big boom.

Chapter Five

Why Theological Mysteries Are Reasonable

We've seen how atheists cannot reasonably deny the possibility of the miracles in the Bible—the God of infinite power can do anything. To know that biblical miracles are impossible requires the omniscience needed to know that God doesn't exist. Our smallness reduces denials of God and His miracles to blind-faith speculation.

We turn now to see how those same limitations make worthless all appeals to theological mysteries to deny God's existence.

The Finite and the Trinity

Great mysteries always confront small people before an infinite God. For example, Scripture teaches that God is a Trinity and that the Christian faith stands or falls on this marvelous truth. But logically reconciling one God existing always as three equally divine persons presents quite a challenge for our limited minds. The best attempts to explain God's triune being with earthly analogies have failed. And as the finite cannot fully grasp the infinite, and the earthly cannot fully depict the spiritual, so we cannot fully grasp and explain the essential nature of the Godhead. "To whom then will you liken God? Or what likeness will you compare with Him?" (Isa. 40:18).

Moreover, no one can know that God as triune is impossible. A God we can fully comprehend is no God, and certainly not the infinite and incomprehensible God of Scripture. Apart from the Bible, to what higher authority can we appeal to say that God can be no greater than what we can understand?

> "For My thoughts are not your thoughts, neither are your ways My ways," declares the LORD. "For as the heavens are higher than the earth, so are My ways higher than your ways,

> and My thoughts than your thoughts." (Isa. 55:8–9)

Atheists who cry "copout" when Christians appeal to mystery fail to admit their own limited abilities, perspective, and knowledge relative to the size of the universe and the boundless perfections of God. If we could fully comprehend God, we would be God. Mysteries must always exist before a limitless God.

> Do you not know? Have you not heard? Has it not been declared to you from the beginning? Have you not understood from the foundations of the earth? It is He who sits above the vault of the earth, and its inhabitants are like grasshoppers, who stretches out the heavens like a curtain and spreads them out like a tent to dwell in. He it is who reduces rulers to nothing, who makes the judges of the earth meaningless. Scarcely have they been planted, scarcely have they been sown, scarcely has their stock taken root in the earth, but He merely blows on them, and they wither, and the storm carries them away like stubble. 'To whom then will you liken Me that I should be his equal?' says the Holy One. Lift up your eyes on high and see who has created these stars, the One who leads forth their host by number, He calls them all by name; because of the greatness of His might and the strength of His power not one of them is missing. (Isa. 40:21–26)

The Finite on the Shore of More Deep Waters

The same applies to the enigma of moral evil in a world created by a perfectly good, all-powerful, and all-knowing God. (The problem of evil will be discussed in detail later.) He has told us that sin began and exists in the will of created beings who freely chose to sin. The blame for sin rests with the sinner. At the same time, God knows all things, including the past, present, and future. How then does He escape liability for sin and its destruction if He knew beforehand that the angels and people He created would sin? Knowing they would fall, why did He make them? Why didn't He place the flaming sword before the forbidden tree, or create mankind without any ability to choose evil? After all, we'll be free in heaven and will never sin.

From our limited perspective, we might conclude that God bears the blame for the sin He hates and condemns. Moreover, Scripture teaches that God knows all things and has foreordained all things, yet remains holy and can never be the direct or indirect author of sin. He judges and condemns sin in perfect righteousness. He holds people fully responsible for their choices.

These are deep waters. Logically reconciling God's perfect knowledge, foreordination, and holiness with human responsibility for sin seems impossible. Yet Scripture clearly teaches them all. Nothing happens beyond God's sovereign control, yet His actions remain morally pure. We alone bear the blame for our sin.

How then should we proceed? Should we join with atheists and skeptics to deny God's perfect knowledge, holiness, or foreordination? Or should we refuse blame for our actions by denying our ability and responsibility to choose according to our own will?

Here, as with the truth of the Trinity, we should first consider our smallness. God's infinite perfections will always confront our weakness with mystery. To deny God's existence and His account of His world and His ways because we cannot fully comprehend them makes our poor frame of reference the supreme standard of truth in and beyond God's universe—an absurdity.

Again, if we could know everything, we would be God. This applies to *all* theological mysteries. Indeed, atheists recognize dark mystery surrounding the life, beauty, order, and immensity of the cosmos. Yet, as if to illustrate how personal preference can override reason, they reject mystery or deem it irrelevant when denying the existence of the God who created and transcends all things, including human reason.

He Has Told Us Enough

And while God has told us all we need to know for life and godliness, He hasn't shown us the solution for every riddle. "The secret things belong to the LORD our God, but the things revealed belong to us and to our sons forever" (Deut. 29:29). Some answers await us in heaven. Some we may never know. In the meantime,

God doesn't ask us to abandon reason to embrace the unreasonable. He doesn't ask that we deny our senses to accept the nonsensical. He does, however, expect us to admit our shortcomings, acknowledge His transcendence, and trust His perfect character.

True wisdom humbly accepts that our finite perspective cannot sit as the final standard of truth in and beyond the universe. We depend on God's word to tell us what we need to know and could never know on our own, even as His word keeps our fallen imagination in check. True wisdom knows that if we cannot know what lies beyond a wall without a look, we cannot know what lies beyond the edge of the cosmos. And if we struggle to grasp what we can see, hear, taste, touch, and smell, how can we speak with authority about things beyond the reach of our senses (apart from what God tells us in Scripture)?

Atheists simply cannot know what they claim to know from their experience of the world. Indeed, the appeal to theological mysteries does far more to affirm our profound limitations before God's infinity, rather than challenging the truth of Scripture or the existence of its Author. We should grant this often-ignored truth before we respond to any claim of unbelief.

The proper approach to all theological puzzles begins with admitting our smallness before God's infinite greatness. Unsolvable mysteries will always confront us. The difficult and seemingly "impossible" truths taught in Scripture reveal our limitations, not problems with God and His word.

Chapter Six

Why Creationism Is Reasonable

Atheists deny God's existence, and therefore deny that He created the heavens and the earth from nothing. But how do they know?

Earlier we saw that no one views the world as a neutral and unbiased observer. We all see things through the colored lens of our most basic beliefs about God, reality, mankind, knowledge, truth, authority, and how we should live. These beliefs (assumptions) form our worldview—the lens through which we see and interpret everything. Those who love the God of Scripture see and accept His fingerprints everywhere. The design, order, and beauty of life and the universe all reflect God's power and genius. Atheists view the same design, order, and beauty as a fluke of time and chance. Believers regard all things as *impossible* without God. Atheists see all things as *possible* without God.

Again we ask, Whose basic beliefs are reasonable? Whose beliefs are justified? Whose beliefs sufficiently explain the design, order, and beauty of life and the universe? And in what object of faith does one trust to form these beliefs? Believers trust God and Scripture. Unbelievers trust their own perspective and opinion.

And note well that "science" doesn't speak—*scientists* speak. Like everyone, scientists are finite, prone to err, and biased. Like us, they view things according to their worldview. To appeal to "science" to judge a matter actually appeals to *scientists* who agree with a given view. And no scientist can speak with authority about ultimate and spiritual things beyond the scope of the scientific method. Further, no scientist—or anyone else—can be a neutral observer of a world that points to God and toward our debt to love and obey Him.

As we've seen, to know that God doesn't exist requires omniscience. And if we cannot know that God doesn't exist, we cannot know that He didn't speak all things into existence. No one can know that God didn't create the earth with light from distant stars already visible, etc. God cannot be constrained by that which He created and sustains. He made the rules, and He can change them.

At the same time, a person of five senses, with limited intellect and the constraints of three or four dimensions, cannot possibly know what a God of infinite power can or cannot do. Apart from God's revelation, we can only guess. And guesswork is not science.

What a Blast

Blind faith trusts that a big explosion and chance created the design and order of the universe, including life and the necessary systems to support it. The scientific method, however, cannot show this. On the contrary, it remains obvious that design requires a designer and that chaos produces nothing but chaos. No scientific discovery proves a world older than the biblical account portrays, unless the data is viewed through the lens of the evolutionary hypothesis, one that requires billions of years.

All things easily fit the biblical account when viewed according to the existence of the infinite God of Scripture. And no scientific data nullifies the biblical account without assumptions that neither the scientific method nor the nature of reality can support. According to the principles of evolution, one might believe that a splendid painting came from a blast in a paint warehouse. But the nature of reality cannot support such a belief. Even the most zealous atheist would view the notion as silly. How then can we know that God didn't create everything from nothing in six days? We can't.

We do well to remember God's rebuke of Job:

> Who is this that darkens counsel by words without knowledge? Now gird up your loins like a man, and I will ask you, and you instruct Me! Where were you when I laid the foundation of the earth? Tell Me, if you have understanding, who set its measurements, since you know? Or who stretched the

> line on it? On what were its bases sunk? Or who laid its cornerstone, when the morning stars sang together, and all the sons of God shouted for joy? (Job 38:2–7)

Reams of excellent scholarship about the age of the universe can be studied to great benefit, such as how the universal flood easily explains the geological properties of the earth. But still vital to the topic at hand—and any related discussion—is this question: How do atheists know what they claim to know? And are the assumptions behind their interpretations of scientific discoveries justified, reasonable, and consistent with the nature of reality? Can such things as chance and the evolutionary process be demonstrated by the scientific method? Can the limited perspective of atheists justify their claims?

For the believer, far more obvious than the brilliance behind an exquisite painting stands the Genius behind all things. But under every unbelieving account of our origins lies a dislike of the truth that God created and owns everything. Unbelief resents that apart from God we have nothing, that His authority is ultimate, that life and every good gift come from Him, and that we owe Him all love, honor, and gratitude—forever. Here we find the reason that people believe unscientific and impossible accounts of the origin of life and the cosmos—they dislike the obvious alternative.

Chapter Seven

Naturalism: The Basics

We turn now to examine the grand presumption underlying "naturalism." Naturalism comes in many flavors, from the absolute claim that nothing can exist beyond matter in space and time, to agnostic versions that grant the unlikely possibility of an immaterial soul, miracles, and the God of Scripture. Opinions vary as to how to define naturalism. But one trait describes every version: They all assume that limited people, from their tiny vantage point, can speak with authority about the ultimate nature of the universe and beyond.

Faith and Delusion

We need not explore every sort of naturalism to see the basic flaw behind them all. To keep it simple, we'll briefly examine a view expressed by the evolutionist Richard Dawkins in his book *The God Delusion*.[1]

Dawkins claims that thought and emotions have a "natural" origin (as opposed to a supernatural or divine origin). The "philosophical naturalist," he says, denies the existence of anything beyond the physical world, including souls, God, and miracles. And while he admits that we have yet to fathom many "natural" things, he hopes one day to know them as part of the natural. One wonders why a "neutral" scientist who claims to follow the facts where they lead would "hope" for such an outcome. Is he admitting his bias? Perhaps his interpretations of the data follow his preferences after all.

Dawkins's faith in human opinion about ultimate realities appears in every flavor of naturalism. The simple and obvious

1. Richard Dawkins, *The God Delusion* (New York: Houghton Mifflin Company, Mariner Books Edition, 2008), 34-5.

question applies to all: How do you know what you claim to know? Or again, how can those who don't know the contents of their neighbor's bedroom without a look know that nothing exists beyond what we can see, hear, taste, touch, and smell? How can every possible thing be limited to what we can experience? Where's the proof? And how big are we compared to the cosmos, let alone what lies beyond it?

Here again, the same people who extol the marvels, mysteries, and immensity of the universe, and thus admit their smallness, can in the same breath assume a divine-like authority and omniscience.

On what ground is naturalism reasonable or scientific? Faithful scientists may limit their conclusions to what they can observe and test. But what justifies the blind leap to define all possible realities and to define what the scientific method has never shown? Naturalism rests on the unscientific and blind-faith notion that limited people, from their limited vantage point and apart from God, can know everything about the universe and beyond. Indeed, one must have the omniscience required to know that God doesn't exist to know that naturalism is true.

Faith and Doubt

In contrast, agnostic naturalists grant that "a god" might exist, that people might have immaterial souls, and that miracles might be possible—but they deny their existence without "tangible" proof. At first glance, this appears more scientific and reasonable than absolute naturalism. A closer look reveals otherwise.

For instance, who views a beautiful painting and requires tangible proof to believe in the existence of a painter? Who visits a bakery and needs tangible proof of a baker? Who lives in a house and requires tangle proof of a builder? No one, in their right mind. Yet what displays more design, complexity, and beauty—and thus more evidence of the existence and genius of its creator: a picture of a flower, or a flower in your garden? A picture of a bear or the bear that destroyed your garbage can? A picture of a baby or a bundle of love whose diaper needs changing?

Some things are self-evident and ridiculous to deny (or

should be). Scripture tells us that all people see and know God's existence, genius, power, and goodness by what He has made. Yet they deny the evidence because it implies our debt to love, honor, and obey Him. People resort to baseless and unscientific opinion to defend their denial of the obvious.

In the end, Scripture tells us plainly that "the whole earth is full of His glory" (Isa. 6:3), a glory so obvious that all people are "without excuse" for not giving God honor and thanks (Rom. 1:20–21). Yet this clearly evident glory is suppressed in unrighteousness (Rom. 1:18), from a human love of darkness and a desire for independence from the ultimate authority of God (John 3:19, Psalm 2:3).

Chapter Eight

Naturalism and Invisible Spirits

We've seen that some naturalists claim that nothing exists except matter in space and time. We turn now to examine an aspect of that view which claims that souls, angels, and God (as infinite spirit) do not exist.

We All Know

We know the reality of angels and the soul because God has told us they exist. Scripture clearly reveals the soul as the essential element of human life, angels as spirits serving those who inherit eternal life, and God as the boundless spirit who created and sustains everything. Each exist beyond the physical realm and possess none of its limitations. And like all things, angels and souls depend on God as their designer, creator, and sustainer.

We also know the existence of the soul by its effects. Deep down, all people know that God exists. His creation, His giving of good things, and our conscience display God's existence and attributes.

> That which is known about God is evident within them; for God made it evident to them. For since the creation of the world His invisible attributes, His eternal power and divine nature, have been clearly seen, being understood through what has been made, so that they are without excuse. (Rom. 1:19–20)

> He did not leave Himself without witness, in that He did good and gave you rains from heaven and fruitful seasons, satisfying your hearts with food and gladness. (Acts 14:17)

God has written His law on every heart (Rom. 2:14–15). In the same way, we know the reality of the soul. Created and sustained by God, and made in His image, we intuitively and immediately see the evidence, apart from complex proofs. The soul appears in personality, in how we love, hate, reason, choose, create, and know good from evil. Time and chance cannot account for such things. Like God, the reality of the soul is obvious.

Sola Materia?

Yet naturalists deny that we have a soul. And while they might be persuaded otherwise, they'll reject God and His word until God changes their heart and they turn from their scorn of Him to see their debt to love and obey Him. But the question remains: How can small people (all of us) know that no spirit animates the human body and lives after death? Naturalists reason from the material to the immaterial, gleaning from the physical that no spiritual world is possible—or at least that it's not how Scripture describes it. But how does this follow? How can the nature of physical things make impossible things that lack physical properties? How can anybody know this?

Like a creature of the sea, concluding from its limited experience and surroundings that nothing exists beyond its realm of salt water, so naturalists deny the existence of a realm beyond the natural.[1] Denying the obvious, they draw conclusions from data that imply no such thing. They point to ice cream to deny the existence of quantum physics, or to a lump of coal to deny the existence of Maine Coon cats.

Children may lack the ability to understand things beyond their capacity, but how much greater is all human ignorance of the universe and beyond? Of course, all things point to the power and genius of God as their creator and sustainer. But the atheist denies this obvious reality and draws conclusions from data that cannot support them. Again, our meager experience and

---

1. C. S. Lewis illustrates this mistaken assumption of naturalists by his allegory of a "mystical limpet" (clam or mollusk) that concludes from its own attributes and limitations that man, who did not share the necessary characteristics of the limpet, such as having a shell, being attached to a rock, existing in water that brings its food, could be nothing more than "a sort of amorphous jelly" of no importance, if he existed at all. From C. S. Lewis, *Miracles* (New York: Harper Collins, Paperback Edition, 2001), 142-3.

perspective reduce the best argument against the existence of the soul to a blind-faith guess.

The same applies to angels. Some deny their existence by appeals to debunked accounts of ghosts and psychics. But these need not provide evidence for angels when the obvious existence of God and His testimony in Scripture suffice. And as angels share none of the properties of the material universe, how can a finite human being know that they don't exist? Every problem we've seen with denials of God's existence apply here also. The understanding and opinion of limited people cannot be the standard of truth or the measure of what can be in and beyond the universe. Such an approach is neither reasonable nor scientific.

Specks of Omniscience?

Again, one must first know that God doesn't exist—an impossibility—to know that angels and souls don't exist. Even so, our ability even to reason about such things points to the existence of God and our soul. Created in His image (though marred by sin), we display finite aspects of God's power and genius. More could be said on this, but the nature of life, humanity, and the self-authenticating and divine nature of Scripture are sufficient for proving the existence of spiritual realities.

Meanwhile the question of how atheists can know what they claim to know remains. On a good day, we might remember where we put the car keys, but we still can't know the contents of our neighbor's basement without a look (or the neighbor telling us). Moreover, what qualifies us—as mere specks in the universe, from the vantage point of standing on another speck in the universe—to speak with authority about ultimate and spiritual things?

Despite the size of the books written by atheists, or the length of their scientific and logical formulas, or the number of people cheering them on (none of whom could exist apart from God), or the fervor of their claims—no argument can show that souls, angels, or God Himself do not exist.

Chapter Nine

The Atheist's Plea: "Entrust Your Eternal Soul to My Opinion"

Earlier we examined the atheists' claim that they stand on reason and science while Christians stand on faith. We saw that all people use reason, and all people have faith in an ultimate authority, though the object of their faith differs. But problems with the atheists' claim run deeper, with an irony we do well to appreciate.

Defining Christian faith as blind, atheists believe they're calling people away from fairy tales to the enlightened facts of science and reason. But beneath this "rational" and "scientific" facade lurks a well-disguised plea—a call to faith. The evangelist of atheism says in effect, "Entrust your meaning, purpose, life, and your soul's ultimate destiny to *my* personal opinion." Or, in short, "Have faith in *me*."

The debate between atheists and Christians has nothing to do with faith versus reason and science. Rather, it contrasts faith in God (who created everything, knows everything, and has explained everything to us in Scripture) with faith in the opinions of people who don't know the contents of their neighbor's attic without a look.

Risky Business

Going beyond their presumed ability to know and explain ultimate realities, atheists also presume the competence to tell others the source, meaning, and purpose of life, including our ultimate destiny. They invite you to trust their insistence on the absence of life after death, of any judgment for our works, and of heaven or hell. They ask you to reject Christ, who offers our only possibility for an eternal, holy, and happy life of meaning and purpose; they ask you to reject and exchange Him for their own speculations. They invite you to deny the obvious, to treat with contempt the One who created us in His image and has given us every good thing—including the ability to reason and discuss such matters. They tempt you to disregard the One who took on Himself infinite suffering that we might have forgiveness of sins and new life. They ask you to discard the knowledge of your God-given purpose, meaning, and destiny of immeasurable joy in heaven as God's royal children in exchange for a few years to do what you want. They entreat you to discard hope and purpose, and instead to accept your life as an accident of time and chance, destined for nothing—even as they ask you to trust them that you won't end up in hell for believing what they say.

Atheists propose a tall story with serious consequences. Yet who would dare to be liable for the eternal destiny of others and direct them to entrust their souls to such blind-faith opinions? Who would write books to influence millions without a certainty that their opinions are absolutely true and not leading people to a horrible fate? Their boldness is frightening, outdone only by their inability to know what they so confidently ask others to embrace. In a telling twist of logic, by denying God's existence they've assumed His place.

Whatever you may think of Pascal's "wager" as an encouragement to pursue God, one should consider the eternal consequences of the Christian versus the atheist being wrong about heaven and hell. The contrast is stark. Eternity is forever. Yet atheists cannot possibly know that hell doesn't exist, and they won't bail you out should they be wrong. And beer commercials aside, there are no parties in that horrible place. Why would anyone risk even a .001 percent chance of spending eternity there? Yet the deceit of sin risks eternal condemnation for a few years of bread that never satisfies (Isa. 55:2), while it incurs the guilt of inviting others to follow this disastrous course.

And as for the here and now, ask any believer if life is better or worse since they've been born again, even with its hardships and scorn of the world. True believers know the infinite value of Christ as compared to the brief and shallow charms of the alternative. Why should anyone put their faith in untrustworthy prophets of the empty and pointless?

The Solid Rock or Sinking Sand

To the believer, God remains infinitely excellent and worthy of our life and worship. To the unbeliever—please reflect upon the ability of your object of faith to meet your needs and deliver on its promises, implied or otherwise. Please consider that appeals to reason and science to reject God are neither reasonable nor scientific. They merely seek to justify unbelief and deny the One to whom we owe all things. All people know that God exists and that He deserves our love, trust, and gratitude (Rom. 1:18–23). And consider those writing thick books that deny the truth of Scripture, who ask you to trust their siren song concerning God and all things. They cannot possibly know what they ask you to believe, and they cannot deliver you if they're wrong. They make money while they offer you nothing and worse in return.

People may find comfort in numbers, but book sales and fame provide a false barometer of truth or virtue, especially today. "The gate is small, and the way is narrow that leads to life, and few are those who find it" (Matt. 7:14). As for the supposed earthly benefits of presuming one's independence from God: "What does it profit a man to gain the whole world, and forfeit his soul? For what shall a man give in exchange for his soul?" (Mark 8:36–37). Gold and large estates lose their value on one's deathbed. In the end, it's a bad tradeoff.

Section Two

Chapter Ten

Introduction to *The Impossibility of God*

I have a book on my shelf entitled *The Impossibility of God.* It's a collection of essays that go beyond claims of a mere improbability of God; the authors argue that "the weight of the evidence is against God's actual existence," and that "the concept of God is logically contradictory." An impressive and weighty book, it contains "most of the important arguments for the impossibility of God that have been published since 1948." The editors challenge readers to "think deeply and critically" about the idea of God, and to ask whether the notion of God is beset with "an ocean of contradictions." Is it "built upon the very idea that disproves it"?[1]

The book's introduction gives a helpful summary of the types of "disproofs" in the book: (1) "an inconsistency in the definition of God"; (2) the inconsistency of God's existence with the existence of evil; (3) inconsistency between an attribute of God and biblical doctrines and events; (4) "inconsistency between two or more divine attributes"; and (5) an inconsistency within single attributes.[2] The authors have thought "deeply and critically" about these topics. Moreover, the intellectual prowess displayed in these essays is impressive and humbling—they're brilliant discussions by brilliant minds.

Arguments, however, stand or fall by the strength of the assumptions on which they rest. A sturdy lighthouse built on sand will not withstand the waves. Ingenious arguments are no exception.

The claims in *The Impossibility of God* deny Him from different angles. And insofar as conclusions follow premises, the

1. Michael Martin and Ricki Monnier, eds., "Introduction," in *The Impossibility of God* (Amherst, MA: Prometheus Books, 2003), 14.
2. Martin and Monnier, "Introduction," 14.

arguments are logically valid. But are the premises true? Or do they rest on the grand presumption we identified earlier? If so, the claims will fail, despite their brilliance. But should the grand presumption go unchallenged, many arguments in *The Impossibility of God* would be hard to refute.

A Review

To introduce the chapters below, let's review the key questions asked thus far:

1. Is God limited to the traits of the cosmos and our limited understanding of logic? Many atheists assume that God, if He did exist, must be limited like us. But how can they know this?

2. Can time and chance account for the amazing design, beauty, and order of life, including every necessary part supporting it? How could this be known, even if we ignore the absurdity and inconsistency of this claim with every known principle observed in the universe (e.g., chaos produces only chaos)?

3. Finally—and the most basic question exposing the grand presumption behind every atheistic argument—do atheists possess enough knowledge of ultimate and spiritual things to speak of them with authority? Can they reduce infinite spirit to formulas on a page? Can they know what lies beyond the universe or the dimensions in which we live? And dare I say it again—do any of them know the contents of their neighbor's hall closet without having a look? (Yes, we'll eventually cover the neighbor's entire house, and maybe the back yard.)

If the answer to these simple questions is no, then what qualifies atheists to speak of things beyond their purview, the greatest being God Himself?

In the following chapters we'll examine the types of arguments presented in *The Impossibility of God* and focus like a laser on their basic assumptions. This is not to dismiss the importance of the details, but merely to show that regardless of the fine points, or the length and complexity of their formulas, claims built on a false foundation cannot stand.

Chapter Eleven

Definitional Disproofs: The Basics

The first type of "disproofs" in *The Impossibility of God* are "definitional." These involve claims that God cannot exist because ideas of Him are logically contradictory. Or simply, the definition of God includes some parts that contradict other parts. (Going forward, I'll assume the biblical definition of God.)

According to the editors, a "definitional disproof" of God looks like this:

1. If God exists, then the definition of God is self-consistent.
2. The definition of God is not self-consistent.
3. Therefore, God does not and cannot exist.[1]

In other words, just as a square circle cannot exist, so any concept of God that contains contrary elements cannot exist.

As believers we certainly agree with the first premise—there are no contradictions in God. He is perfect and cannot be a mix of conflicting attributes. But what about the second premise—that the definition of God isn't self-consistent? And does the conclusion that "God does not and cannot exist" necessarily follow? Could what we deem a problem with the definition of God be no more than a problem with our limited understanding?

The Argument Expanded

Specific contradictions alleged by the authors will be addressed in later chapters. For now, we ask if the limited perspective of the atheist can establish the claims. Several assumptions lie behind the above argument, including the ever-present belief in the ade-

1. Introduction to "Definitional Disproofs of the Existence of God," *The Impossibility of God* (Amherst, MA: Prometheus Books, 2003), 17.

quacy of the atheist to know things beyond the realm in which we live. If we take into account our limitations, perhaps a more complete version of the above argument would be as follows:

1. If God exists, then the definition of God is self-consistent.
2. The definition of a perfect and infinite God who transcends all things is not self-consistent, according to people so limited that they cannot know the contents of their neighbor's guest room without a look, and who don't know what lies beyond the dimensions of our existence, and cannot possibly know transcendent realities.
3. Therefore, God cannot exist in or beyond the universe unless the finite minds of people, from their grossly limited perspective, can fully grasp and logically reconcile every element of the definition of God.

Of course, the revised version sounds quite unreasonable compared to the original. Yet the revision rightly takes into account human limitations. Given God's infinite greatness, many things about God are difficult to understand and reconcile in the human mind. We cannot possibly know that God can be no higher than what we can logically reconcile in our thoughts. Again, mystery is both logical and to be expected when the finite explores the infinite. If we could fully comprehend God, He wouldn't be God. We can know of Him only what He has chosen to reveal to us.

The Counter Argument

We do better to admit our smallness before an infinite God than to adopt the irrational notion that our limited minds and reasoning form the final standard of truth in and beyond the universe. Perhaps we could offer another argument, as follows:

1. God is infinite spirit.
2. Finite people who forget where they put the car keys and have a brain smaller than a soccer ball cannot possibly know that an infinite spirit cannot exist or what He could do if He did.

3. Therefore, every claim that God cannot exist constitutes guesswork of no value in describing realities beyond the severe limits and defects of human understanding.

Again, my version lacks brevity, but what it lacks in economy it redeems with truth. For instance, how can logic used by limited people explain the nature of an infinite spirit? Logic orders our reasoning, but it cannot disprove the transcendent. It gives atheists no powers beyond those of mere mortals. And again, to know what is possible in and beyond reality as we know it requires knowledge of everything in the universe and beyond. Logic provides no such knowledge. And while the contributors to The Impossibility of God are certainly brilliant, they suffer from the same constraints as the rest of us.

I would be remiss if I didn't add that no book which denies God could be written without Him. People can deny God only because He exists. Chaos produces chaos, not life, reason, and authors. Of course, this assumes that God created and sustains us, along with the universal laws that enable us to discuss such things. But I leave it to the reader to weigh the alternative—that products of chaos, in a world founded on chaos, could observe, analyze, and interpret random products of chaos, give opinions, and trust the opinions of other products of chaos.

We do better to acknowledge what Paul told the people of Athens about God:

> He Himself gives to all life and breath and all things; and He made from one, every nation of mankind to live on all the face of the earth, having determined their appointed times, and the boundaries of their habitation, that they should seek God, if perhaps they might grope for Him and find Him, though He is not far from each one of us; for in Him we live and move and exist. (Acts 17:25–28)

God has made Himself known and given us life and reason that we might use them for His honor and our good.

Chapter Twelve

Definitional Disproofs: God as Virtuous

We turn to a specific example of a "disproof" where the definition of God is said to contain logically contrary features, making Him impossible. According to Douglas Walton, a perfect God must be virtuous. But virtue—as defined by the ancient Greeks and accepted in "ethical theory"—requires human imperfections. Human imperfections, however, are incompatible with divine perfection; therefore a perfect and virtuous God cannot exist, Walton concludes. And he views this argument as "dialectally powerful" because the conclusion follows "plausible" premises. Moreover, the idea that God cannot be both perfect and virtuous, using a definition of virtue derived from "ethical theory," has "become the official theological view," according to Walton.[1]

The "Official" View

To begin, I should note that this "official" view, at least outside the ancient Greek context, is best applied to *human* virtue. And while some may have elevated the definition to an unchangeable and absolute axiom applicable also to God, you won't find such a definition applied to God in the historic creeds and confessions, nor throughout history among those who believe the Bible to be God's word and who believe the basic doctrines of Christianity. Nor will you find this view among philosophers and unbelievers who admit their limitations and understand that applying such things to God is nothing more than undue speculation.

1. Douglas Walton, "Can an Ancient Argument of Carneades on Cardinal Virtues and Divine Attributes Be Used to Disprove the Existence of God?" *The Impossibility of God* (Amherst, MA: Prometheus Books, 2003), 38-40.

The Bible's View

Scripture teaches that God is perfect in every conceivable way. He is holy, good, and righteous. His virtue, therefore, is perfect. "No one is good except God alone" (Mark 10:18). "There is no one holy like the LORD" (1 Sam. 2:2). "The Rock! His work is perfect, for all His ways are just; a God of faithfulness and without injustice, righteous and upright is He" (Deut. 32:4). "The LORD our God is righteous with respect to all His deeds which He has done" (Dan. 9:14).

By contrast, Walton's chosen definition of virtue requires "overcoming pains and danger," suffering, and the risk of being destroyed in struggles to defeat opposition and enemies—things contrary to the Bible's description of God as eternally perfect and omnipotent. Moreover, God is the source and measure of true virtue, subject to no standard beyond Himself.

Walton's argument says little more than that a perfect God with imperfect attributes is a contradiction. Agreed. Or that a God who is both perfect and imperfect at the same time cannot exist. Also agreed. Or that a perfect God doesn't meet the Greeks' or Walton's "official" definition of virtue. Agreed, again. Or that the God of the Bible isn't like Greek gods. Indeed, every believer would agree. But does it follow that because the God of Scripture doesn't meet a Greek or human definition of virtue, He cannot exist? Does it follow that the only possible God is a human and or flawed God? How can Walton know such a thing? (He can't.) Is defining God away really as easy as picking a definition of some flawed attribute of humanity, requiring that God must meet that definition, then declaring that the biblical God doesn't exist because the Bible says He's perfect?

Perhaps the "virtue" argument might have been useful to the ancient Greeks where mythical "gods" were made in the image of depraved people. Or maybe it could be redone to show that a perfect God cannot logically be an extension of flawed mankind, thus affirming the biblical contrast between God and imperfect humanity. But whatever its merits, the "virtue" argument says nothing about the impossibility of God as He has revealed Himself in Scripture.

A Vital Concession

Walton admits "that there appear to be epistemological limits about what can be known by human thinkers on the basis of logical reasoning about the nature of the Divine being."[2] Quite true. And while we can applaud this honest concession, Walton has overlooked his own "epistemological limits." He has failed to apply what he knows of other "human thinkers" to his own virtue argument.

When we struggle to logically reconcile what Scripture teaches about God, our lack of understanding cannot serve as the final standard of what can be true. We remain infinitely small, a blip in time, a speck in the cosmos, unable to speak of transcendent realities apart from what God has revealed. Atheists and believers alike have trouble admitting our smallness before a boundless God, but Isaiah's words still apply:

> Who has directed the Spirit of the LORD, or as His counselor has informed Him? With whom did He consult and who gave Him understanding? And who taught Him in the path of justice and taught Him knowledge, and informed Him of the way of understanding? Behold, the nations are like a drop from a bucket, and are regarded as a speck of dust on the scales; behold, He lifts up the islands like fine dust. Even Lebanon is not enough to burn, nor its beasts enough for a burnt offering. All the nations are as nothing before Him, they are regarded by Him as less than nothing and meaningless. (Isa. 40:13–17)

Weak children of dust lack the vantage point and knowledge to define away the infinite God of Scripture, Greek philosophy notwithstanding.

2. Walton, "Ancient Argument of Carneades on Cardinal Virtues and Divine Attributes," 42.

Chapter Thirteen

Definitional Disproofs: Omniscience, Goodness, and Moral Agency

We come to our second example of a "definitional disproof." Here, a God of such excellence that He deserves worship cannot coexist with human moral agency.[1] Drawing from the moral philosophy of Immanuel Kant (1724–1804), James Rachels contends that you cannot be a moral agent unless you follow the moral dictates of your own heart. But to be a worshiper of God requires complete submission to *His* moral dictates. An all-powerful, all-knowing, and all-wise God deserves worship and total obedience. But since worshipers view God as the supreme authority to be worshiped and obeyed, they give up their autonomy as moral agents. Total submission is contrary to the independent decision-making required of a moral agent. Therefore, no such God exists.

Rachels' essay opens with Kant's well-known jab, "Kneeling down or groveling on the ground, even to express your reverence for heavenly things, is contrary to human dignity." While problems with calling worship "undignified groveling" will become clear below, here's the basic argument:

1. If any being is God, he must be a fitting object of worship.
2. No being could possibly be a fitting object of worship, since worship of such a one would require others to abandon their role as an autonomous moral agent.
3. Therefore, there cannot be any being who is God.[2]

1. James Rachels, "God and Moral Autonomy," *The Impossibility of God* (Amherst, MA: Prometheus Books, 2003), 45-58.
2. Rachels, "God and Moral Autonomy," 54.

Worship and Free Moral Agency

Does viewing God as worthy of worship and total devotion abandon our ability to make moral choices according to the preference of our will? Does bowing the knee to God's excellence and supreme authority annul our ability to make free moral choices? Again, if moral autonomy consists merely of the independent authority to determine absolute rules of right and wrong, Rachels presumes what he intends to prove, as noted above. But if "moral autonomy" involves the ability to make moral choices according to the preference of our will, do we abandon "moral autonomy" in a blind "suspension of our own judgment" when we freely choose to worship God?

A Heart to Choose God

Rachels notes that "the first commitment of a moral agent is to do what in his own heart he thinks is right."[3] But what if the moral agent thinks it is right to worship and obey God? Rachels admits that in some cases it would be reasonable for a moral agent to "blindly" follow the judgment of those with greater knowledge and wisdom. But if a moral agent can follow others in *some* cases, why not in *each* case where another has superior knowledge and wisdom? And if that knowledge and wisdom are always perfect, why not choose to follow in every case? To do otherwise would be foolish. By the author's own reasoning, complete trust in a faultless God would constitute the best choice for a free moral agent. Scripture tells us that the freest moral agent has a heart to choose the greatest good. And what greater good exists than God, the source and definition of good? Why would a rational believer choose otherwise?

Rachels responds to this objection by claiming that it "rests on a misunderstanding of the idea that (necessarily) God is perfectly good," and that we cannot know if a being is God without first knowing that His commands are perfect, and therefore that He is perfect. But in principle this avoids the claim that the existence of God is incompatible with free moral agency. If God is perfect,

3. Rachels, "God and Moral Autonomy," 54.

freely choosing His will constitutes the best choice, and thus His existence remains compatible with free agency. If He isn't perfect, He's neither God nor a fit object of worship, and thus the argument doesn't apply, given that the author's first premise describes God as "a fitting object of worship."[4]

God's Freedom and Human Dependence

Second, on what basis can Rachels assume that if God deserves worship and submission to His will, then He couldn't also create humanity with a free will to choose whether or not to worship Him? Given our human limitations, how can anyone possibly know with certainty that God could not create free moral agents who depend on Him for the definition of good and evil, and whose worship of Him constitutes the right response to His goodness and infinite excellence? Perhaps we're meant to be dependent moral agents, and a presumed independence from God is a bad idea—especially in light of our human limitations.

Apart from Scripture, does Rachels have access to higher principles of the universe and beyond to which all of reality, including God Himself, must conform? As it is, Scripture makes clear that God created and sustains all things and cannot be subject to principles outside Himself.

The Moral Agent's Object of Faith

Third, the claim implies in effect that free moral agency requires faith in our own opinion (not faith in God) as the final moral authority. Believers and unbelievers both reason by faith in an ultimate authority, and both make moral choices as they please. At issue is not moral agency per se, but rather which object of faith and ultimate authority is justified, trustworthy, and adequate to determine right and wrong. Atheism requires trust in an authority that can't know the contents of his or her neighbor's living room without a look. Biblical freedom, however, gives the ability and right to choose and trust the best authority, which is God and His word. Rather than destroying free moral agency, submission to God's authority allows and empowers people to

4. Rachels, "God and Moral Autonomy," 55.

choose the greatest good.

"Moral" Agency?

Fourth, why speak of "moral agents" when no absolute standards of right and wrong exist in a world without God? Free moral agency, absent divine moral standards, involves billions of opinions on what constitutes right and wrong, with none more qualified than another to act as the final judge. Morality becomes relative. Indeed, finding an ultimate judge of right and wrong poses quite a problem in a world where life somehow showed up and progressed by random mutations and survival of the fittest. What authority does one limited and pointless random chance accident have in telling other limited and pointless random chance accidents what must be right and wrong in a pointless random chance universe?

For example, what absolute standard condemns the strong killing the weak, when according to the hypothesis of evolution the death of the inferior improves the gene pool and advances the species? People acting "according to precepts" they can "conscientiously approve in their heart,"[5] who fear no eternal judgment for their behavior, can "conscientiously approve" anything. Of course, atheists have morals, and most atheists would strongly condemn murder and the application of survival of the fittest to humanity. But since an atheistic worldview provides no ultimate moral authority and standards, atheists borrow their ethics from the worldview they deny.

God's Purpose and Prerogative

Finally, Scripture says that God created us for His glory. Such is His prerogative. And having given us all things, we owe Him worship and loving obedience to His will. Therefore God's existence *does* bring "unlimited authority and an unlimited claim on one's allegiance." But how does that render the response of worship "contrary to human dignity"?

Perhaps ingratitude and disrespect toward a superior would

5. Rachels, "God and Moral Autonomy," 55.

constitute the greater indignity, while being created in God's image to participate in His eternal plan involves a dignity beyond that of random accidents with no ultimate point or purpose.

In the end, this disproof merely denies that a God who deserves our utmost love, loyalty, and obedience can exist because He doesn't fit Kant's notion of the human will as supreme. This claim says little more than that some people find it beneath their dignity to bow the knee to their Creator. And it may be that Adam and Eve agreed with that long ago—when in a proto-Kantian elevation of their "human dignity" above the One who gave them life and every good thing, they sinned and brought death and destruction on the world. To call love and fidelity to God "groveling" says far more about Kant's heart than the nature of God and reality.

To conclude, we all serve a master. We may serve our own passions, wants, and opinions, or the winds of the prevailing culture, or other man-made gods. Or we can serve the good and just God of the Bible. Whatever our choice, it has no effect on God's existence. Our thoughts, formulas, syllogisms, and the beliefs behind them do not determine or alter ultimate reality. God doesn't go away because someone exalts personal autonomy over His sovereign glory and purpose for us.

Kant was certainly brilliant. But like the rest of us, he didn't know the content of his neighbor's kitchen without having a look.

Chapter Fourteen

Deductive Evil Disproofs: The Problem of Evil and Rational Support

We come to the second category of arguments against God's existence, what the editors call "deductive evil disproofs," or variations of "the problem of evil."[1] The present chapter provides some helpful background, while subsequent chapters will address specifics.

In general, denials of God built on the problem of evil enlist the same irrational assumption that underlies and undermines every argument against God—that finite and fallen people can speak with authority, without God's explanation, about things infinitely beyond them. Mystery, the limits of human understanding, and unproven or unjustified premises will also demonstrate how logical and theological riddles need not worry believers. We'll also see how appeals to the problem of evil to deny God display the unbeliever's need of the gospel of Christ.

In the opening paragraph of the first "evil disproof," the author portrays belief in God as unsupportable and irrational—embracing that which our own beliefs disprove.[2] We'll see, however, that belief in God is logical and reasonable. Also, I'll examine the mistaken notion that deductive proofs provide the greatest evidence for the existence of God. Logic remains necessary and important for right thinking, yet most things are known without a process of deductive reasoning, and often with greater certainty than a logical argument can provide. Knowing how and why this is so will clarify the nature of knowledge and proofs, why belief is reasonable, and why unbelief is without excuse.

1. J. L. Mackie, "Evil and Omnipotence," *The Impossibility of God* (Amherst, MA: Prometheus Books, 2003), 59-124.
2. Mackie, "Evil and Omnipotence," 61.

Again, underlying all denials of God is the belief that the minuscule can speak with authority about the ultimate, infinite, and spiritual. Alongside this stands the notion that what we cannot understand or logically demonstrate cannot exist or be true. In other words, reality in and beyond the universe is reduced to what we can comprehend. Atheists seem unaware or unwilling to admit that their entire enterprise stands on such an unreasonable idea. And as we'll see, this belief governs every expression of the problem of evil as evidence against God's existence.

Therefore, any serious discussion of God's existence should always consider the assumptions behind the claims and recognize the severely limited vantage point from which people speculate about ultimate realities. And again, every argument built on irrational, unjustified, or false assumptions is unsound. Further, in approaching such a difficult issue, we do well to consider the enormous depth and breadth of what we have yet to know of life and the universe, let alone what lies beyond it. True wisdom admits its limitations, including our approach to the problem of evil.

Chapter Fifteen

Deductive Evil Disproofs: The Problem of Evil and Proof

In the first of the essays in *The Impossibility of God* that appeal to moral evil as proof of God's impossibility, J. L. Mackie claims that belief in God lacks "rational support," and that people must reject reason and ignore the conclusive arguments against Him in order to believe. The "problem of evil," according to Mackie, is one such argument. A logical problem, it basically says that if God has infinite power and can easily eliminate evil, and if He's perfectly good, He would always want to eliminate evil—but since evil exists, God must either be less than infinitely powerful or less than perfectly good, or both.[1]

An in-depth discussion of the nature of knowledge is beyond the scope of this book, but for our present purpose, knowledge is justified belief, or belief supported by sufficient proofs and evidence. The contributors to *The Impossibility of God* contend that belief in God lacks justification and thus cannot be knowledge, while logical arguments prove that God cannot exist.

But do logical arguments provide the best proof to know whether or not God exists? A few simple illustrations will indicate that logical proofs or disproofs fail to provide the highest or most justified knowledge. Nor do they even represent the way people typically know things.

A More Certain Knowledge

For example, if you happen to be a married man like me, let me ask you this: When you first met your wife, did you run calculations

1. J. L. Mackie, "Evil and Omnipotence," *The Impossibility of God* (Amherst, MA: Prometheus Books, 2003), 61-62.

on her facial features, with color charts and measurements of the symmetry of the nose to the eyes, and from all that deduce that she was pretty? I hope not. More likely, you saw, you swooned, and the rest is history. (As for how our wives first perceived us, perhaps they were given a kind of blindness.) In any case, people know beauty intuitively and immediately, without a process of logical reasoning or deduction. Seeing is believing.

And when you eat a piece of chocolate, do you logically deduce whether or not it tastes good? No. You bite and you know intuitively and immediately whether it's delicious. Tasting is believing.

How then does this apply to the knowledge of God's existence, especially since He isn't physically present with us?

Imagine a trip to a museum with some friends, where beautiful sculptures, paintings, and inventions fill the rooms, and delectable baked goods fill the racks of the first-floor bakery. No artists are present, most having departed centuries ago. Now ask yourself, would anyone viewing the exhibits need a series of logical arguments to determine the existence of the sculptors, painters, and inventors of the items on exhibit? No. The existence and genius of the creators are intuitively and immediately known by the genius of their works. In fact, such knowledge gives more certainty of their existence than any logical argument could ever provide. Seeing is believing (and knowing). In the same way, no one visits a bakery and logically questions the baker's existence when a cupcake provides evidence enough, and no one needs a deductive argument to know for certain the origin of croissants.

You may be familiar with the pre-Socratic philosopher Zeno's many logical arguments that motion is impossible. Philosophers still debate whether these arguments have ever been sufficiently refuted.[2] Yet regardless of the brilliance of his arguments (and they are brilliant), we intuitively and immediately know that

2. Perhaps the most familiar of Zeno's arguments posits that to move from point A to point B, one must first pass through a mid-point C. But before arriving at C, one must pass through another mid-point D. As time is finite, and there are an infinite number of mid-points, one could never traverse an infinite number of mid-points and thus never go from point A to point B. Motion, then, is impossible. See Frederick Copleston, S. J., *A History of Philosophy*, vol. 1, *Greece and Rome* (New York, NY: Image Books, 1993), 56-57.

motion exists. Likewise, it might be difficult to logically prove the existence of a rock on which we stub a toe, though we'll intuitively, immediately, and painfully know its existence with great confidence.

As with sculptors, painters, inventors, and bakers, we know the existence and genius of God by the genius of His works—known intuitively and immediately, apart from deductive arguments. In fact, we have infinitely more evidence for God as our creator than for the creators represented in the museum or bakery. We live immersed in the brilliance of His handiwork everywhere and in everything, including our minds and the ordered reasoning by which we contemplate such things. We live in a world where a single cell makes our greatest works look like child's play. The obvious evidence for God in His works give infinitely more proof than the best logical arguments, while logical "disproofs" cannot annul such knowledge any more than Zeno can annul the existence of motion. Yet people deny what stares them in the face because they don't like the implications:

> For since the creation of the world His invisible attributes, His eternal power and divine nature, have been clearly seen, being understood through what has been made, so that they are without excuse. For even though they knew God, they did not honor Him as God, or give thanks; but they became futile in their speculations, and their foolish heart was darkened. (Rom. 1:20–21)

Indeed, they hate the implications:

> This is the judgment, that the light is come into the world, and men loved the darkness rather than the light; for their deeds were evil. For everyone who does evil hates the light, and does not come to the light, lest his deeds should be exposed. (John 3:19–20)

Reasonable and Obvious

Nothing said here signals a retreat to the irrational and the illogical to defend faith in Christ and Scripture. On the contrary, how could anyone rationally attribute the brilliant design, order, and operation of the universe—including the marvels of life, thought, feeling, personality, and relationships—to an accident of time and chance, a random bolt of lightning in a random primal soup on a random planet in a random universe? Such a conclusion represents the epitome of irrationality and blind-faith speculation. By comparison, a library as the product of ink and woodchips in a hurricane appears reasonable.

Knowing the existence of the artist from the genius of his art and the existence of God from the genius of His works contradicts nothing of logic and rationality. Some things are just plain obvious.

Finally, this brief foray into the nature of proof and knowledge does not suggest that the problem of evil cannot be sufficiently answered. Quite the contrary. In the next chapter, we'll begin examining the problems of using the "problem" to deny God. The existence of moral evil in human hearts and human choices poses no problem for God's existence and a healthy Christian faith.

Chapter Sixteen

Deductive Evil Disproofs: More Problems with the Problem of Evil

We now turn to a few problems with "the problem of evil" (moral evil, for our purposes). Again, the claim says that if God has infinite power He can easily eliminate evil, which is what He would always want to do if He's perfectly good—but since evil exists, God must be less than infinitely powerful or less than perfectly good, or both.[1]

From our narrow human perspective, evil poses a logical puzzle and raises difficult theological questions. The problems vanish, however, if God is reduced to being less than perfectly powerful or good, or if the meaning of "good" is changed, or if we redefine "evil" as less than absolute wickedness or as a necessary means to greater good. Such "solutions" are unnecessary, however. And besides, they avoid the essential problem. Moreover, any attempts to defend belief in God by distorting biblical truth will dishonor God and Scripture. They'll only affirm the unsound assumptions behind atheistic arguments.

Deficient Remedies

We can agree that "attempts to sidestep the problem" fail. For instance, it contradicts Scripture to think of evil as the necessary flipside of good, or as necessary to produce greater good. God is not only independent of all things, He remains the source and definition of good. He has no need of evil for anything. Also, moral evil began in the will of created beings and exists nowhere else. It is temporary and will be banished, while perfect goodness

1. J. L. Mackie, "The Problem of Evil," *The Impossibility of God* (Amherst, MA: Prometheus Books, 2003), 78-81.

will remain forever. Indeed, an ounce of corruption would ruin heaven. Moreover, we don't live in the best of all possible worlds. Every life would improve by one less sin.

Trimming God's attributes—such as reducing God's power and knowledge—would solve many logical puzzles of the Bible. But such "answers" merely affirm a self-defeating defense—the claim that the God of perfect power, goodness, and knowledge cannot exist. Scripture teaches that God's power and knowledge are infinite. God knows everything always, even the free and future acts of angels and people. And though philosophers cry "impossible," God can do anything. He can create a world where people make free choices for which they are blamable, even while He knows beforehand what they'll choose. This may not satisfy our limited grasp of logic, with our points on a temporal or logical continuum. Yet who can know that an infinite God who transcends our meager thoughts of time and logic could not create such a world of free people? Here again, the objection boils down to this: "If I cannot understand or logically reconcile a scenario in my mind, then that scenario cannot exist." Deep thinkers, however, would do well to admit their limits. They would do even better to stop imposing them on God.

God can indeed bring good from evil. He sometimes uses our sinful choices (for which we're blamable) to accomplish His perfect will. But to think of God as *dependent* on evil destroys His glory. And God condemns doing evil that good may result (Rom. 3:8). God *did* bring infinite blessing from infinite evil in the crucifixion; He can turn the worst of Satan's evil schemes to good. Indeed, God conceived, planned, and orchestrated Christ's voluntary death, as the apostle Peter proclaimed to a gathered crowd in Jerusalem:

> This Man, delivered up by the predetermined plan and foreknowledge of God, you nailed to a cross by the hands of godless men and put Him to death. (Acts 2:23)

Yet Christ's murderers bear the blame for their willful and unforced sin, as Jesus confirmed:

> For the Son of Man is to go, just as it is written of Him; but woe to that man by whom the Son of Man is betrayed! It would have been good for that man if he had not been born. (Mark 14:21)

As noted earlier, God's sovereign control and human responsibility for sin present a theological difficulty. But as we'll also see concerning moral evil, it poses no ultimate problem for the believer. God's infinite wisdom and power can bring good from evil while He remains righteous. And He needs nothing to accomplish His will—least of all evil.

True Freedom

Proposed "solutions" to this "problem" include the idea that the good of human freedom to choose evil outweighs the risk of its terrible results. Or that a truly free will requires the choice between evil and good. But while these concepts place responsibility for evil in the will of created beings—where it belongs—they distort true freedom. Scripture speaks of a new freedom, including the freedom to choose good, not the old "freedom" to choose evil. "If…the Son shall make you free, you shall be free indeed" (John 8:36).

Indeed, we'll be most free in heaven without evil, while God is perfectly free and has never had the inclination or option to choose evil. Just as dining out cannot be enhanced by adding poison to the restaurant's menu, true freedom is not improved by the option to choose evil.

God *could* have created a universe of free people without the possibility of evil—but He chose not to, and He did not ask for our advice beforehand (Job 38:4, Isa. 40:13–14).

Familiar Assumptions

The same faulty assumptions behind other atheistic arguments occur here. For instance, could God have allowed evil for reasons we cannot fully comprehend? Yes. Do we lack complete understanding of an infinite God and His ways? Yes again. But for the atheist appealing to evil to deny God's existence, the answer appears to be *no*. They say in effect that what we fail to understand cannot exist or be true, thus elevating their reasoning to the place of highest authority in and beyond the universe. God's ways, however, are infinitely above our ways (Isaiah 55:8–9), and mysteries must abound. We know that God will eliminate evil forever. But He will do so according to His perfect plan, at a time known only to Him.

Again, we are tiny, God is not.

> It is He who sits above the vault of the earth, and its inhabitants are like grasshoppers, who stretches out the heavens like a curtain and spreads them out like a tent to dwell in. He it is who reduces rulers to nothing, who makes the judges of the earth meaningless. (Isa. 40:22–23)

How can people of five senses and three or four dimensions know what an infinite God would or could do apart from what He reveals to us? Are atheists reasonable in making their limited perspective the ultimate standard of what can exist in and beyond the universe? Are things rendered impossible because we cannot understand them? Such leaps of blind faith reflect the refusal by atheists to acknowledge mystery and their own smallness, even as they presume for themselves a kind of omniscience. Apart from God's revelation, no one can know what defines ultimate good, or know that a perfectly good God would never allow people the freedom to choose evil. God alone determines such things. We know them only by what He has revealed in Scripture, and by what He has actually done in the world.

Reasonable Claims

Consider a small sample of logical arguments, the first of which summarizes the main point of this book:

1. To know that an infinite God doesn't exist requires knowledge of everything in the universe and beyond.
2. People don't know the contents of their neighbor's bathroom without having a look.
3. People cannot possibly know that God doesn't exist.

Or the following as applied to the problem of evil:

1. To know that a good God would never allow evil requires knowing every possible reason why He would or would not do so.
2. We have trouble remembering why we went downstairs, and we lack the infinite knowledge required to know every possible reason why God might allow evil.
3. Finite human beings cannot possibly know that God's existence is impossible, because they don't understand why He would allow evil.

The atheist denies rational support for belief in God, yet we look in vain for any rational support for limited people speaking with authority about ultimate and transcendent realities. God's existence is obvious, regardless of the deductive arguments people devise to explain Him away.

Responsibility, Blame, and Redemption

Blame for moral evil lies with the evildoer. Indeed, most atheists readily admit responsibility for their choices, even as they enjoy God's blessings and assert their freedom to choose good or evil as they please. They defend their freedom with a vengeance. Yet in order to explain God away, they assume that a God of perfect power and goodness could not create people with the ability to choose between good and evil. But would they prefer that God had created them without the freedom to make choices for which they're responsible? If not, why use the consequences of that freedom (i.e., evil) to deny the God who gave it to them?

Thankfully, God has remedied evil and our guilt at infinite cost to Himself, providing the escape from condemnation and the path to eternal life. He did this through Christ's perfect obedience to satisfy His standard of righteousness, and by His death to pay the penalty for our sin. In the infinite excellence of God, displayed in the person and work of Christ, we therefore have every reason to love and trust God in the face of great mysteries, including the problem of evil. As the "secret things belong to the

LORD our God" (Dt. 29:29), so belongs the answer to why God created us when He knew we would freely choose to sin.

Chapter Seventeen

Thoughts on Pain and Natural Evil

Thus far, we've addressed the problem of *moral* evil, or the sin that exists only in the will and choices of created beings. We turn now to a brief discussion of *natural* evil, or earthly calamities such as tornadoes, earthquakes, hurricanes, birth defects, disease, death, and the like—along with the pain and suffering they produce.

The horrors of earthly suffering cannot be avoided or denied. If you've never asked *why*? through a veil of tears, you have yet to experience life on earth. From the loss of a loved one, the torture and murder of millions at the hands of tyrants, or the terrible results of a flood, a fire, or bacteria—people suffer. Atheists point to natural evil, such as children suffering from horrific diseases, to reject belief in a God who would cause, allow, or fail to prevent such things. Because the theological, philosophical, and practical issues involved are complex and profound, this brief chapter will barely scratch the surface. Nonetheless, it answers the vital question that applies to this and all objections to God's existence: Can anyone *know* that God cannot exist because pain and evil exist?

The Background to Natural Evil

Scripture blames the free choice of created beings for sin, bringing separation from God, spiritual darkness, and the curse of natural evil. Sickness, natural disasters, and death had their beginning in the world by sin. Rebellion against God spoiled paradise and brought a curse upon the world. Since then, "All have sinned" (Rom. 3:23), and every human being enters this world with Adam's guilt and sinful bent (Rom. 5:12–14). We've all treated God with contempt, and we rightfully deserve His judgment. God would be just to condemn us all.

He can do whatever He pleases with what He created and

sustains. He owns everything. He owes us nothing, while we owe Him everything, and every good that we enjoy comes from His gracious and merciful hand. "Who are you, O man, who answers back to God?" (Rom. 9:20).

A Reasonable Question

God is righteous in all His judgments, and none can rightly accuse Him of unrighteousness because we suffer. We live and breathe by His mercy. At the same time, God is good, gracious, merciful, and overflowing with lovingkindness. Being just, He neither rewards wickedness nor punishes innocence. But babies yet to utter a bad word die in their parents' arms, while others never leave the womb before meeting the scalpel of one sworn to do no harm. (Sadly, many who point toward evil to deny God's existence make a virtue of killing the unborn.) Many suffer under the policies and actions of evil rulers, while those rulers appear to suffer the least. Psalm 73 laments the favorable circumstances of the wicked as compared to the relatively righteous.[1] We can therefore sympathize to some extent with unbelievers' questions about the existence of an all-powerful and all-good God when evil and suffering run rampant in His creation. Believers and unbelievers alike face great mystery in all of this.

An Unreasonable Conclusion

Does mystery concerning the nature and extent of suffering in the world justify the conclusion that God cannot exist? The previous chapters highlighted the inability of atheists to know and explain ultimate and spiritual realities, and the fact that human limitations reduce their claims to guesswork and blind faith in a presumed ability to know what they cannot possibly know. We've noted that atheists would need infinite knowledge to know that the infinite God doesn't exist, that the Bible's miracles are impossible, that nothing exists beyond what we experience with our senses, and that God didn't speak all things into existence in six days.

1. Of course, the writer of Psalm 73 adjusted his attitude when he saw God's ultimate judgment of the wicked (verses 16–28).

In a similar way, to know that pain and natural evil exclude God's existence, one would need to know what the atheist cannot possibly know. For instance, the atheist would need to know that we don't exist forever after death, that temporary suffering cannot have an eternal purpose beyond what we presently understand, that God will not execute justice and render to evil people their just deserts in the hereafter, that no rewards and punishments will be given in the next life to compensate for what people do or suffer in this life, that evil will never be remedied and destroyed, that mankind is not responsible for moral evil and the curse that brought natural calamities, that God cannot righteously judge and curse the world because of sin, that He is unjust and mankind deserves better, and that His word is false and doesn't explain all we need to know about pain and evil. The atheist cannot possibly know such things, and Scripture denies them all. No one can possibly know that the presence of moral and natural evil in the world makes the existence of a good God impossible.

In God's response to Job, He exposes the nature of a human heart that questions His goodness and justice in the face of suffering in the world. "Will you really annul My judgment? Will you condemn Me that you may be justified?" (Job 40:8). So before we criticize God, we should consider Job's response to this: "Behold, I am insignificant; what can I reply to Thee? I lay my hand on my mouth" (Job 40:4). Created, dependent, and fallen people cannot judge or make claims on a perfect God.

God's existence doesn't depend on our limited perspective and understanding. His ways are infinitely higher than our ways—in history, in our personal circumstances, and also in human suffering. Here again, to reject God's existence because we don't understand such suffering makes our limited understanding the standard of what can exist or be true, which is an unreasonable notion. Ultimate reality cannot be determined by the limited perspective and knowledge of people who still don't know the contents of their neighbor's den without a look (I'm running out of rooms!) Dismissing an infinite and holy God because we don't understand the existence of pain and evil is foolish. As it is, Scripture tells us all we need to know about it.

God has displayed His goodness in "satisfying your hearts

with food and gladness" (Acts 14:17). He "causes His sun to rise on the evil and the good, and sends rain on the righteous and the unrighteous" (Matt. 5:45). He has made His power and glory known to all by what He has made (Rom. 1:18–20). And greatest of all, He displayed His infinite excellence and moral perfection in the person and saving work of Christ, through his life, death, and resurrection. Evil exists—but God has remedied it, and He will ultimately dispose of it forever. Indeed, "The sufferings of this present time are not worthy to be compared with the glory that is to be revealed to us" (Rom. 8:18).

A Greater Evil

While mysteries abound, our limited perspective about them determines nothing about God. In the end, all unbelief rejects God's obvious existence and authority from a desire to do whatever we want. Ironically, no greater evil exists than to deny and insult the One who created us, who gives us all good things, and who has willingly paid the price of infinite suffering for us that we might be holy and happy forever. We enjoy His blessings of love, family, food, friends, and the stars in the sky, but we use our God-given talents to insult and reject Him. Moreover, those who point to pain and evil to deny God should consider how they encourage evil (and the additional suffering it brings) by telling people they'll never be judged and condemned for it. Yes, evil exists, but none so terrible as contempt for the One to whom we owe all love, honor, and gratitude. Such contempt leads others down a terrible road. Jesus said,

> Whoever then humbles himself as this child, he is the greatest in the kingdom of heaven. And whoever receives one such child in My name receives Me; but whoever causes one of these little ones who believe in Me to stumble, it is better for him that a heavy millstone be hung around his neck, and that he be drowned in the depth of the sea. Woe to the world because of its stumbling blocks! For it is inevitable that stumbling blocks come; but woe to that man through whom the stumbling block comes! (Matt. 18:4–7)

A Great Comfort

If you're a believer who cries with the psalmist, "When shall I come and appear before God? My tears have been my meat day and night, while they continually say unto me, Where is thy God?" (Psalm 42:1–3)—know that the day will come when God does this:

> He shall dwell among them, and they shall be His people, and God Himself shall be among them, and He shall wipe away every tear from their eyes; and there shall no longer be any death; there shall no longer be any mourning, or crying, or pain; the first things have passed away. (Rev. 21:1–4)

Be encouraged and pray for those that oppose your faith in Christ. May God give grace that they might embrace Christ through faith, in whom is true and everlasting life—in whom is no evil.

Chapter Eighteen

Doctrinal Disproofs: God's Test of Adam and Eve

We turn now to "doctrinal disproofs" presented in the book *The Impossibility of God.* These are claims that certain teachings or acts of God in Scripture contradict what Scripture teaches about God's attributes. Richard R. La Croix, in "The Paradox of Eden," argues that God's test of Adam of Eve in the garden of Eden was unjust. Therefore, righteousness cannot be an attribute of God.[1]

According to La Croix, when God told Adam and Eve to abstain from the tree of the knowledge of good and evil, they either knew or did not know that disobedience to God's command was evil. If they knew, then they already had the knowledge of good and evil, and so the command to abstain from the forbidden fruit would have been "an inadequate and unfair test" of their righteousness. God would have known beforehand that they wouldn't be easily tempted to eat because they would have known they had nothing to gain from it—so He was unjust to put them to the test. On the other hand, if Adam and Eve lacked the knowledge of good and evil, they could not have known that ignoring God's command was evil. God would be unjust to test them and punish them for disobedience. Either way, God would not be righteous in putting Adam and Eve to the test.

They Knew More Than Enough

To begin, Scripture teaches that Adam and Eve were created without the particular knowledge of good and evil imparted by the forbidden fruit. Yet they knew God's command and the

1. Richard R. La Croix, "The Paradox of Eden," *The Impossibility of God* (Amherst, MA: Prometheus Books, 2003), 127-8.

penalty for disobedience. They also knew that God made them and gave them all good things. They knew they needed God to know His will, their purpose, and how they should live. They also understood that God was good and trustworthy. Adam and Eve had every reason to reject the serpent's lies. They knew more than enough to obey God, and to expect severe punishment if they treated His goodness and authority with contempt.

Therefore, knowledge of God's will, goodness, trustworthiness, and ultimate authority—combined with the threat of death—gave a sufficient basis for God's test of Adam and Eve's devotion. Yet this knowledge differed from the knowledge of good and evil the forbidden fruit would impart. La Croix merely assumes that the banned knowledge of good and evil was necessary for the test, when they had reason enough without it. In making his case, La Croix ignores the context and purpose of the trial, the details revealed in the text, and our dependence on the text to know the meaning of the event. Like God's accuser in the first chapters of Job, he discounts that God's excellence and authority provide ample ground for a proper love, honor, and obedience to God.

Scripture's account of creation, the fall, and redemption tells us about the origin of sin and about our need of a Savior. The foolishness, ingratitude, and self-exalting nature of sin stands in stark contrast to the perfect power, goodness, righteousness, and authority of our perfect God. And while the exact nature of the knowledge imparted by eating the forbidden fruit is beyond our scope and unnecessary to answer La Croix's argument, we easily see the difference between the loving relationship of Adam and Eve with God prior to their sin, and the separation and enmity thereafter. The merging of a depraved heart with the knowledge given by disobedience made for a terrible union in the soul—and a disaster for humanity.

In the end, the Creator, Sustainer, and Giver of all good things, to whom we owe all things, can design a trial of obedience any way He sees fit—without consulting us. And even if we could find no human basis for such a trial, we still lack sufficient knowledge to question His perfect wisdom in bringing the trial to us. We're just too small. As God questions us through the apostle

Paul, "Who are you, O man, who answers back to God? The thing molded will not say to the molder, 'Why did you make me like this,' will it?" (Rom. 9:20).

A Greater Problem

The first chapters of Genesis present a far greater problem than the imagined scenarios of La Croix. Scripture presents a solution impossible with human beings and possible only with God (Luke 18:26–27). How can sinful people escape God's judgment when He cannot compromise His justice, and when "every transgression and disobedience received a just recompense" (Heb. 2:2)? How can God remain just and save the souls of guilty rebels? We'll present the answer in detail in chapter 30—after exploring more "disproofs" from *The Impossibility of God.*

Chapter Nineteen

Doctrinal Disproofs: Immoral Judgments

In his essay "A Moral Argument for Atheism," Raymond D. Bradley claims that God doesn't exist because His actions in the Old Testament and His judgment of sending sinners to hell are grossly immoral.[1] According to Bradley, Satan only committed a few misdemeanors; he violated none of the moral principles that God violates, and he represents a "paragon of virtue" compared to God.[2]

Suggesting points of agreement with theists, Bradley affirms the existence of objective moral principles. He claims to reject the idea that truth is relative, or that individuals or "counting heads" (i.e., popular vote) can determine the truth of "moral judgments." He then presents five moral principles on which he believes atheists and theists can agree—and goes on to claim that the God of the Bible has violated them all.

Moral Principles?

Before we examine God's alleged corruption, we should first question the source of this author's moral principles by which he condemns God. Again, we ask, does his worldview provide a basis for ethics? Absent God, we are products of time and chance. Our life and ability to discuss right and wrong evolved from a single cell, and somehow progressed by "natural selection" to the present discussion.

So where did the author's "objective moral principles" come

1. Raymond D. Bradley, "A Moral Argument for Atheism," *The Impossibility of God* (Amherst, MA: Prometheus Books, 2003), 129-146.
2. Bradley, "A Moral Argument for Atheism," 141-142.

from? Did the author (himself an accident of time and chance) derive right and wrong from his own opinion? Or does he take his cue from other accidents of time and chance? Either way, he's guilty of the relativism he claims to reject.

Without God as the source of objective morality, what remains beyond his view and the views of others? And who qualifies as the ultimate judge? One random fluke of chaos stands equally as unqualified to determine moral absolutes as another. Thus, the cultural relativism that pervades atheistic thinking applies equally to personal morality. Lacking an ultimate authority, no absolute standard exists to judge the morality of individuals, cultures, or God.

And again, how does evolution give us right and wrong? How does an alleged process built on the destruction of the weak by the strong become the morality of the strong protecting the weak? How does that which destroys the evolutionary means by which life and the gene pool improve become an absolute moral principle? "Moral" tigers and crocodiles starve to death.

In the opening line of his introduction, the author quotes a character in Dostoyevsky's *The Brothers Karamazov*: "If there is no God, all things are permitted." He then dismisses the quote as myth, with no apparent justification. All agree that people make laws and punish those who break them. But time and chance produce no moral absolutes or ultimate accountability. And what evolutionist can tell headhunters and despots they're morally wrong if they survive at the expense of their weaker neighbors? Is it any wonder that eugenics—the cleansing of the gene pool to advance the human race—immediately preceded the Holocaust? Had Germany won World War II, and by their account defeated the weak, to what absolute moral principle could evolutionists appeal to condemn Hitler's atrocities?

When people dethrone God as the ultimate moral authority, all that remains is personal preference and the tyranny of those with the most power to inflict their desires on everyone else. Dostoyevsky was correct.

Relativism and Borrowed Moral Principles

While the author claims to reject a relativistic basis of morality—that of personal preference or head counting—he can't avoid it. Evidence for this peppers his essay: "on my view," "as almost everyone would agree," "as I see it," "I want to say," "I take to be objectively true," "I want to say," "I would like to think," "If I am right," to cite a few examples. Rejecting God, Bradley can appeal only to his own opinion or the opinion of others, the very relativism he claims to reject.

Again, none of this denies that atheists have well-defined morals. They've likely been raised with remnants of a Christian worldview permeating their laws, culture, and parents. And all people have standards of right and wrong, because God created us in His image and has written His law in every heart and conscience (Rom. 2:14–15). Time, chance, and survival of the fittest do not produce "Thou shalt not kill" (Ex. 20:13, Dt. 5:17 KJV), or "Love thy neighbor as thyself" (Lev. 19:18, Matt. 19:19 KJV), or "Inasmuch as ye have done it unto one of the least of these my brethren, ye have done it unto me" (Matt. 25:40 KJV). Atheists, it seems, presume God and moral standards in order to criticize and explain Him away. But whether God is guilty of violating the moral principles He has given to us, as claimed by the author—let's see.

Chapter Twenty

Doctrinal Disproofs: Common Moral Ground

In "A Moral Argument for Atheism," Bradley assumes common moral ground with believers and presents five "paradigms of objective moral truths" that he believes both atheists and theists would consider morally wrong: 1) the intentional murder of innocents, 2) giving women to soldiers as sex slaves, 3) making people cannibalize others, 4) human sacrifice, and 5) endlessly inflicting agony on others for their beliefs. Calling them "our" moral principles, the author claims that God's actions in Scripture have violated them all. Christians must choose between an unholy God or a false Bible.[1]

The present chapter suggests a proper starting point to respond to this and other atheistic claims and to show why atheists are unqualified to make those claims. Subsequent chapters will critique specific elements of the above argument.

Incompatible Moral Ground

In the previous chapter, we observed that Bradley's claim to reject moral relativism rings hollow. His worldview gives no basis for objective morality and reduces to individual or collective preference. Time, chance, and survival of the fittest produce no moral absolutes. And despite his attempt at common ground with theists, the atheistic and Christian worldviews remain incompatible. Christians derive moral absolutes from God's law—both written on the heart of every person and revealed in Scripture—and deny that objective truth or morals can exist apart from God. The

1. Raymond D. Bradley, "A Moral Argument for Atheism," *The Impossibility of God* (Amherst, MA: Prometheus Books, 2003), 132-134.

atheist must borrow from our worldview to agree with us on any moral principle.

Bradley, however, claims that moral principles exist without God, to which all people—as well as God (should He exist)—are subject. Christians reject this and believe that all moral principles come from God. And except for moral evil (found only in the will of fallen angels and people), God created all things and can never be subject to a higher principle outside Himself. Atheists might assert that God's actions are contrary to what Scripture teaches about His perfect moral character and what He requires of us. But the atheistic worldview, of itself, gives no standard by which to criticize anything, let alone God.

"There is no God besides Me; it is I who put to death and give life. I have wounded, and it is I who heal; and there is no one who can deliver from My hand" (Deut. 32:39). The Old Testament reveals many instances of God directly or indirectly killing entire cities, nations, and even the entire human race (Noah and his family excepted). Indeed, every death, including infants and children, traces to God's judgment of sin in the garden of Eden. Death entered the world by Adam's sin. Does the Bible then affirm the author's claim that God's actions show Him as unholy or Scripture as untrue? Should God be viewed with "abhorrence" as a murderer of innocent people, as Bradley suggests?

Every judgment of God, including the eternal punishment of souls in hell, should terrify any thinking and feeling person—believer, atheist, or otherwise. "Behold then the kindness and severity of God" (Rom. 11:22); "It is a terrifying thing to fall into the hands of the living God" (Heb 10:31). But while God's judgments are dreadful and sometimes unfathomable, are they unholy? More to the point, can limited, fallen, and self-justifying people know enough to discredit what Scripture says of God's perfect knowledge, holiness, and righteous judgments? What would the atheist need to know to justify such a claim?

A Proper Context and Perspective

To answer these and all ultimate questions, we return again to our beginnings. God the Father, God the Son, and God the Holy

Spirit have existed forever. They need nothing and created all things from the overflow of divine goodness. Apart from God, we have nothing. Every good thing we enjoy comes as a gift from His gracious hand. To God we owe all love, honor, and obedience—always—while God owes us nothing, not a single breath.

> He Himself gives to all life and breath and all things; and He made from one, every nation of mankind to live on all the face of the earth, having determined their appointed times, and the boundaries of their habitation. (Acts 17:25–26)

God is the potter, we are the clay. He gives and takes away, and He can do with His own as He pleases. "Alas, who can live except God has ordained it?" (Num. 24:23). "In Thy book they were all written, the days that were ordained *for me*, when as yet there was not one of them" (Psalm 139:16). This forms the starting point and basis for a proper understanding of ourselves and a proper humility to approach difficult theological questions. "The fear of the LORD is the beginning of knowledge" (Prov. 1:7).

A proper view of our smallness and dependence on God for all things, including knowledge of realities beyond our limited perspective, should make us humble, reverent, and silent before God's severe lessons and judgments.

Knowledge of Every Relevant Fact?

How then does our knowledge compare to God's infinite knowledge? He knows everything, including the past, present, and future into eternity. He knows every heart and every relevant detail that comes before His throne of justice. God sees what we cannot see and knows what we cannot know. Do we possess sufficient knowledge to sit in judgment of God's deeds?

For instance, God determines the birth and death of every person. He can also give everlasting happiness to a soul He separates from physical life in infancy or old-age. Can we know that God will fail to make all things right in the end, or unjustly decide the eternal fate of any soul? Do we possess sufficient knowledge to correctly judge a single case? Atheists can only guess, even as they presume to exhaust every possible explanation in and beyond the universe with a three- or four-sentence syllogism. Unless we can know the eternal fate and every relevant fact concerning souls that leave this physical realm, we cannot possibly know that God is unjust in any of His judgments.

For the recipients of God's grace in Christ, our present sufferings—including an "untimely" death—are not worthy to be compared to future, eternal, and immeasurable happiness (Rom. 8:18). Indeed, "If we have hoped in Christ in this life only, we are of all men most to be pitied" (1 Cor. 15:19). We cannot properly evaluate our short life apart from a proper consideration of eternity—something God knows intimately, and something atheists cannot possibly know apart from God's revelation. Eternity matters. Apart from eternity, nothing matters.

As atheists embrace the irrational notion that their limited perspective defines the ultimate standard of what is possible in and beyond the universe, so they also embrace the irrational notion that their limited understanding forms the ultimate standard by which to judge the righteousness of God's actions.

Chapter Twenty-One

Doctrinal Disproofs: Double Standard

Can a holy God can do what unholy people cannot? And can God use sinners as instruments of His judgments against sin?

As instruments of His chastening and justice, God often uses fallen people—whether Israel as God's instrument to carry out His sentence on evil people in the Promised Land, or wicked Babylon coming over the hill to chasten apostate Israel. Is God unjust in doing Himself what He tells us not to do? By wiping out the Canaanites, does God legitimize the atrocities of a Hitler or Stalin?[1]

Having supposedly identified "moral principles" by which God and mankind are bound, Bradley claims that no "double standard" can rightly exist for God and people. He states, "If it is good enough for God, it must be good enough for us."[1] Throughout his essay, Bradley blurs or eliminates the distinction between the Creator and the creature and denies that different standards of behavior could apply to each.

Unequal "Authorities"

As we noted earlier, no standard of right or wrong exists apart from God. He isn't subject to any authority above and beyond Himself. Moreover, He does whatever He pleases with what He created and owns, and He does so in perfect knowledge, holiness, justice, and wisdom. To Him we owe everything; apart from Him we have nothing. And every good thing we enjoy comes from His gracious hand. We depend on God for everything and are

1. Raymond D. Bradley, "A Moral Argument for Atheism," *The Impossibility of God* (Amherst, MA: Prometheus Books, 2003), 132-134.

infinitesimally limited in knowledge, perspective, and wisdom by comparison.

Yet in response to His infinite goodness, we disregard and insult His authority, seek our own way, and deny His obvious power and genius in and about us. We treat with contempt the infinite suffering of Christ on the cross to pay the penalty for our sin and purchase for us eternal life and happiness. Apart from God's direction, we cannot be trusted to always act with moral purity.

Contrary to Bradley's claim, never could a double standard be more proper than here. We are not God.

> For I am God, and there is no other; I am God, and there is no one like Me, declaring the end from the beginning and from ancient times things which have not been done, saying, "My purpose will be established, and I will accomplish all My good pleasure." (Isa. 46:9–10)

Indeed, the pursuit of our pleasure, while ignoring God, created our troubles and the need for God's judgments in the first place.

Also, can God choose for Himself a special people to honor above others? Yes, He can do what He wants with what He owns. Concerning Israel we read,

> The LORD did not set His love on you nor choose you because you were more in number than any of the peoples, for you were the fewest of all peoples, but because the LORD loved you and kept the oath which He swore to your forefathers. (Deut. 7:7–8)

And can God use a sinful people ("all have sinned and fall short of the glory of God," Rom. 3:23) to execute His judgments on wicked nations? Yes, and without our permission:

> It is not for your righteousness or for the uprightness of your heart that you are going to possess their land, but it is because of the wickedness of these nations that the LORD your God is driving them out before you, in order to confirm the oath which the LORD swore to your fathers, to Abraham, Isaac

> and Jacob. Know, then, it is not because of your righteousness that the LORD your God is giving you this good land to possess, for you are a stubborn people. (Deut. 9:5–6)

God is the creator; we are not. God is the judge of the universe; we are not. God always judges in righteousness; we lack perfect knowledge and pervert justice.

When the prophet Habakkuk pleaded with God to remedy the gross wickedness of Israel, God answered—and the Babylonian armies came over the hill to conquer. Israel was decimated. Harsh, you say? Yes. Undeserving? No. And we lack the infinite knowledge to know otherwise. Not until the next life will we fully understand the evil of treating our perfectly holy and good Creator and Benefactor with contempt.

But what about the fate of precious little ones suffering under the consequences of the wickedness of others? We recognize and cringe at the terrible results of sin, but we entrust their souls to a God of perfect goodness and holiness, whose spotless justice will be clearly displayed and vindicated in eternity. Until then, we have the witness of Christ suffering the penalty of infinite wrath in our place to maintain His justice in saving sinners. Thus we can trust His perfect goodness to do what is right with every soul, especially precious children (including those in the womb).

Holy Might Makes Right

Does God's judgment of evil justify people committing evil, as Bradley claims? Does "might make right" for sinful leaders to violate God's law to butcher millions of people, including the unborn, to advance those leaders' personal power, pleasure, or ideology? No. They will be eternally condemned for their murders. God has assigned government and law courts to judge lawbreakers while Western jurisprudence stands on principles found in Scripture. But a human judge, to whom the law gave authority to pass a death sentence where the penalty fits the crime, doesn't give license for others to murder. How does it follow that the punishments of the holy and perfect Judge of all give license for evil?

Moreover, the author has failed to distinguish between the infinite perfection of God as the judge of all (who knows every facet of every case, including the heart, and who always judges rightly) and the limited perspective of His sinful and guilty creation. God can judge where we cannot. And when He does, sinful and limited people cannot possibly know that His judgments are unjust. We simply cannot fathom everything God sees, and we cannot know for certain the eternal recompense and destiny of those God judges. Every account will be fully settled in eternity.

Here, as everywhere, a right view of the infinite excellence of God contrasted with our self-justifying and utter smallness renders worthless the many denials of God's existence, including those addressed here. God says, "You thought that I was just like you; I will reprove you" (Psalm 50:21). The holy Creator of all life stands qualified to judge, and He answers to no one—while finite and fallen creatures possess no such ultimate authority, even as God has provided us the principles by which to punish criminals and protect the innocent. Despots who violate those principles will pay a severe price for it. And while much can be said concerning the inadequacy of moral arguments against God, people lacking God's omniscience are unqualified to make them.

Chapter Twenty-Two

Doctrinal Disproofs: Eternal Torment

We've seen that a double standard for the Creator and His creatures is proper and necessary. Holy omniscience always judges in perfect righteousness. As the source of all good, He cannot be judged by a standard outside Himself. We, however, depend on God's revelation for truth, knowledge, and all moral principles. So is God evil because He has broken the "objective moral principle" which states that "it is morally wrong to torture people endlessly for their beliefs"?[1] Is God unjust to send people to hell?

People believe lies, and people make mistakes. But to spend eternity in torment for some innocent but false religious belief would be a great injustice. Agreed. But God's condemnation of sin, including the sin of unbelief, bears little resemblance to the author's indictment of God for sending people to hell. And while we cannot fully grasp the justice of such a severe punishment, we must ask why God imposes it, and why Scripture deems it an appropriate penalty for sin.

The Context and Crime

We return again to our starting point. From the overflow of His infinite goodness, God created us in His image that we might enjoy Him as His beloved children. Every good we enjoy comes from Him. He reigns as the supreme authority, the source and sustainer of all things. To disobey Him, to refuse Him His due, to reject His authority and exult our personal desires over His perfect and sovereign will—these things constitute a hateful insult.

1. Raymond D. Bradley, "A Moral Argument for Atheism," *The Impossibility of God* (Amherst, MA: Prometheus Books, 2003), 132-134.

To neglect a life of thanksgiving to God displays awful ingratitude. To refuse to worship God betrays His love as we set our affections elsewhere. To treat with contempt the God of infinite holiness, majesty, and goodness embodies an evil we can scarcely comprehend. Indeed, "The heart is more deceitful than all else and is desperately sick; who can understand it?" (Jer. 17:9). Sin involves wickedness so profound that only the infinite suffering of Christ can fully pay its deserved penalty.

God does not condemn anyone for the mere mistake of believing the wrong thing, but for disdain of His perfect authority, character, and goodness. Moreover, God also punishes contempt toward His infinite love and mercy toward us in the person and saving work of Christ. The idea that God condemns people for a mere intellectual mistake, as our author contends, grossly distorts unbelief and God's response to it.

Without Excuse

Also, note well that guilt for contempt toward God's character and authority precedes the guilt of rejecting Christ as Lord and Savior. By this we can better understand how God can judge those who have never heard the gospel. The rejection of Christ constitutes a great evil, but does not form the first and only basis of God's damnation of sinners. People who scorn God's authority and goodness prior to hearing the gospel have already incurred God's judgment. Indeed, all are without excuse:

> For the wrath of God is revealed from heaven against all ungodliness and unrighteousness of men, who suppress the truth in unrighteousness, because that which is known about God is evident within them; for God made it evident to them. For since the creation of the world His invisible attributes, His eternal power and divine nature, have been clearly seen, being understood through what has been made, so that they are without excuse. For even though they knew God, they did not honor Him as God, or give thanks; but they became futile in their speculations, and their foolish heart was darkened. (Rom. 1:18–21)

All people know enough to incur blame for their response to God and their willful choice of who they trust and worship as their supreme authority. (Again, all people have an ultimate object of faith and worship.) And as we've seen, God will deal justly with infants, babes in the womb, and all who appear to lack the capacity to turn from evil and seek God. What appears to be unjust in this life will be made right in the next—and atheists cannot possibly know otherwise. God will judge all people with perfect justice in eternity. And eternity is all that matters in the end.

God has so displayed His power, goodness, and genius that all people are responsible to seek Him, honor Him, and love Him. Ingratitude, irreverence, or infidelity toward God, or the exulting of our desires over God's will—all are without excuse. Indeed, God has written His law on every heart (Rom. 2:14–15), and He has provided sufficient evidence that we all can trust His perfect justice in the face of mysteries and theological difficulties. Christ suffered infinite wrath to maintain divine justice, that He might extend mercy to sinners. Since God cannot corrupt His righteousness to save a single soul, and since He upheld perfect justice at infinite cost to Himself, we can trust that no soul will go to hell who doesn't deserve to be there.

Not the Last Word

Atheists, however, assume the wrongs of our short time on earth to be the last word, denying that God can rectify the evils of this life in the next. Yet no human being can possibly know such things. And apart from God's grace and power, no argument or evidence will convince anyone who refuses to bow the knee to His obvious authority, genius, and goodness. May God have mercy to open the spiritual eyes of any who would lead others down that perilous road.

Chapter Twenty-Three

Doctrinal Disproofs: Bible Difficulties

As we proceed, we do well to remember that true wisdom begins with the fear of the Lord (Prov. 9:10). Wisdom admits its weakness and dependence on God for all things—including knowledge. The importance of applying this basic truth to every aspect of life cannot be overstated. Indeed, "When I am weak, then I am strong" (2 Cor. 12:10). In the face of God's infinite excellence and power, we cannot rightly view the world, ourselves, our circumstances, or God Himself without a proper and heartfelt understanding of our smallness.

David's Census

This vital principle applies to how we approach theological and textual difficulties in Scripture. For instance, in Raymond D. Bradley's "doctrinal disproof" essay that we've been considering, [1]he claims that differences between the two accounts of the same census taken by David indicate an error in Scripture (2 Sam. 24:1 and 1 Chron. 21:1–7). The first passage says God was angry with Israel and incited David to number the people. The second says that Satan incited David to do so. In either case, God judged David and thousands died as a result. Bradley concludes that the accounts are contradictory and that God unjustly condemned David for what He incited David to do. Admittedly, the two passages pose a challenge for the best of interpreters. But whatever the solution, a proper view of our human limitations—the flipside of a necessary reverence of God's greatness—must precede every approach to Scripture.

1. Raymond D. Bradley, "A Moral Argument for Atheism," *The Impossibility of God* (Amherst, MA: Prometheus Books, 2003), 132-134.

A Presumed Error

According to Bradley, Bible difficulties easily point to errors, because God doesn't exist. Men wrote it, and men make mistakes. Moreover, some who profess belief in Christ and in the authority of Scripture accept many of its moral principles as true, but dismiss historical details as either inaccurate or metaphors designed to display spiritual principles.

Yet when atheists and "liberal" Bible interpreters appeal to "error" as the default response to difficult problems, they ignore their own human limitations. They presume to know every possible explanation, even those known only to God. For atheists, this reflects their unjustified faith in a supposed ability to know and explain transcendent realities from their limited human perspective (apart from God's explanation). Professing believers who reject the accuracy of portions of Scripture unwittingly (maybe wittingly) affirm the unbelieving assumptions behind wholesale rejections of Scripture as God's word.

Viable Explanations and the Wise Approach

Scripture provides several examples of how the two passages about David's census can be reconciled. For instance, who caused Job's suffering? God, Satan, or both? God was the ultimate catalyst, while He allowed Satan to put Job to the test. Such a scenario could easily explain the accounts of both God and Satan inciting David to number the people. Since God was angry with Israel (2 Sam. 24:1), He could have allowed Satan to be His means to chasten both David and the nation. Moreover, God's judgment of David for doing what He incited him to do has a parallel in His hardening Pharaoh's heart to prevent him from releasing Israel before Egypt could be completely destroyed. God justly prevented Pharaoh from acting in self-interest to escape judgment, knowing that Pharaoh still regarded God and His people with contempt. And since God sees the heart, Pharaoh would have remained guilty of hostility toward God even if he had released God's people before the last of the ten plagues. God merely prevented Pharaoh from saving Egypt and his own skin by not allowing him to let the people go. Pharaoh deserved the blame for his sinfulness.

Returning to David's census, the first passage tells us that "the anger of the LORD burned against Israel" (2 Sam. 24:1), but neglects to say why. As God observed the hearts of David and the people, perhaps He saw sinful pride and trust in the earthly power of their armies. Perhaps David *wanted* to take inventory of his earthy resources, but refused to act for fear of the consequences. God may have used Satan to incite David to do what David wanted to do but was afraid to do. Perhaps God desired an outward display of the inner sin by inciting David's suppressed desire into action, teaching David and Israel a lesson in the process. Perhaps there are better explanations. But regardless, we know for certain that we lack sufficient knowledge to conclude that no possible solution exists. Our resources are too limited to conclude that Scripture is in error.

Advances in our understanding of history, archaeology, theology, and other fields have solved many so-called errors in Scripture. At the same time, true wisdom will study, wait, and admit that the answer may elude our grasp. Wisdom also admits our great limitations when we face profound difficulties and mysteries. Wisdom understands that we see dimly until we see clearly in glory. Wisdom knows its smallness before an infinite God and shuns conclusions that deny His authority. And wisdom depends on God for all things—including answers to difficult questions. "The secret things belong to the LORD our God, but the things revealed belong to us and to our sons forever" (Deut. 29:29). Believers hold fast to the things revealed and leave the secret things where they belong—with God.

A proper approach to Scripture requires a proper humility before the God who wrote it. "Let no man deceive himself. If any man among you thinks that he is wise in this age, let him become foolish that he may become wise" (1 Cor. 3:18). "To this one I will look, to him who is humble and contrite of spirit, and who trembles at My word" (Isa. 66:2). A proper humility goes a long way in approaching the difficulties of Scripture.

Chapter Twenty-Four

Doctrinal Disproofs: Do Miracles Deny the Possibility of God?

We come now to "doctrinal disproofs" involving miracles.[1] Before presenting her own unique claim, Christine Overall presents claims that "miracles" do not point to God as their source. Viewing these as "a step in the right direction," she goes further and says that miracles give positive evidence that the God of Scripture *cannot* exist. I'll respond to her first three arguments below, then in the next chapter offer a critique of her claim that miracles actually give evidence *against* God's existence.

In and Out of Time?

To begin, a common argument against the biblical description of God asserts that if He exists, He could not simultaneously dwell both *in* and *beyond* space and time. Therefore, since God is said to exist beyond space and time, He could not be the cause of miracles occurring in space and time.

We as human beings do not live both in and beyond time and space. Does it necessarily follow that God is like us in that respect? Do our human limits, or what we know of time, space, and matter, imply such limits in God? Atheist apologists and philosophers offer this claim as fact. Yet the only way we can know what an incomprehensible and infinite spirit can be or do is by what He condescends to reveal to us. As it is, He has told us in Scripture that He simultaneously exists and operates both in and beyond space and time. At best, this first argument presented by Ms. Overall affirms that we are not divine, even as those mak-

1. Christine Overall, "Miracles as Evidence Against the Existence of God," *The Impossibility of God* (Amherst, MA: Prometheus Books, 2003), 147-153.

ing it presume omniscience to make the claim. Again, no finite person, apart from God's revelation, can possibly know what an infinite spirit can be or do. To do so argues from blind faith.

Special Versus Regular Works of God

Next, the author claims that if God causes every event, it makes no sense to say He "specially caused" any particular event (such as a miracle). Or if He causes "special" events, then He cannot be the cause of "regular" events. Yet why can't God organize reality according to regular events (such as by natural laws), and then also create a special event at a particular time and place? Scripture teaches both. God can do whatever He wants, whenever He wants. And again, who can know enough to say otherwise?

At best, this argument presented by Ms. Overall highlights problems with believers distinguishing natural versus supernatural events when everything in the universe operates by the ongoing exertion of God's power. Nothing operates "naturally" apart from "the word of God's power" (Heb. 1:3). This includes miracles. Imprecise language and a lack of appreciation for the miraculous nature of "regular" events do not preclude God from creating, sustaining, and then parting the Red Sea.

Unknown Source of Contemporary Miracles

Another argument claims that no miracle can be assigned to a specific agent without our knowing the distinct pattern of how the agent has operated in the past, such that how it will operate in the future can be predicted. And if an action can be predicted, it comes under "scientific law" and cannot be considered a miracle. Therefore, if miracles are unique and unpredictable, they cannot be assigned to God or any other agent. In other words, if you view a "miracle," you cannot know for sure that God performed it.

This argument has merit when applied to contemporary accounts of miracles. We cannot always know that a miracle was performed by God. Satan and his deceptive minions use signs, wonders, and other good things to divert us from Scripture to trust in mere experience. So-called miracles give credibility to false teachers, false religions, and the occult. Many "miracles" have natural explanations. Some are fake, some imagined. Yet their circumstances might point to God. Maybe they follow a prayer or a particular need. Even so, we cannot know the source of an apparent miracle today with the same confidence we have with the miracles recorded in Scripture. Our perspective and conclusions are suspect, but God's word is not.

Therefore, this argument doesn't apply to the miracles in Scripture. God has clearly revealed when and why He has performed them, even if they could not have been predicted. Moreover, violations of natural law agree with the God who created and sustains all things. "Behold, Thou hast made the heavens and the earth by Thy great power and by Thine outstretched arm! Nothing is too difficult for Thee" (Jer. 32:17). Miracles are kid's stuff for God. And He who makes the rules can change the rules as He pleases, even for a moment.

Despite its merits as applied to accounts of contemporary miracles, the argument poses no threat to God's existence or to the authority of Scripture, where the nature, timing, and purpose of God's miracles in biblical history are revealed. Moreover, God's ability to easily perform miracles appears in the design, creation, and ongoing operation of the universe. Again, the God who can create and sustain all things from nothing can do anything.

Faith and Contemporary Signs

In the end, true faith doesn't rest on reports or the experience of contemporary miracles. If we need a sign to believe in Jesus Christ, we have yet to humble our heart to recognize the infinite excellence of God in created reality and in the person and saving work of Christ as recorded in Scripture. And while God may use many things (including miracles) to get our attention, saving faith comes when God opens our spiritual eyes to see the beauty of His holiness, the ugliness of our sin and its deserved penalty, and the infinite excellence and sufficiency of Christ as our substitute and Savior. He alone satisfied God's just penalty for sin in His death on the cross; He alone met the requirement of perfect obedience for eternal life. Therefore we boast in the gospel of Christ, "for it is the power of God for salvation to everyone who believes"

(Rom. 1:16). God can certainly perform miracles, but we need not see one to believe in Him.

Chapter Twenty-Five

Doctrinal Disproofs: Do Miracles Disprove God?

Having critiqued three claims that miracles do not imply God as their source, we turn to a fourth argument from Christine Overall, one that is counterintuitive. She says that "permanently inexplicable" violations of "natural law" not only fail to imply God as their agent, but they give positive evidence that the Christian God does not exist. She suggests that miracles are inconsistent with what a benevolent, all-powerful, and all-knowing God would do.[1]

Miracles as "Disharmony"

To begin, Ms. Overall notes that believers view the "harmony" of the universe as evidence for God. But since miracles disrupt that harmony—they're a "moment of chaos," or metaphorical "dissonance"—they cannot be evidence of God. Christians, she says, cannot have both harmony and chaos as evidence of God. But we must ask: Do God's miracles in Scripture represent chaos? And does Scripture teach that God must always act a certain way at all times?

Scripture teaches that all things display God's genius, power, and goodness. His miracles throughout history, including those in Christ's ministry, display His control over everything. Thus, Jesus giving sight to the blind to show His divine credentials as Messiah agrees with the character of a good God. His raising the dead and walking on water display not "chaos" or "dissonance," but God's power and genius in ordering His universe as He sees

1. Christine Overall, "Miracles as Evidence Against the Existence of God," *The Impossibility of God* (Amherst, MA: Prometheus Books, 2003), 147-153.

fit. When Christ calmed the chaotic storm of the sea, the amazed disciples said, "Who then is this, that He commands even the winds and the water, and they obey Him?" (Luke 8:25). We can safely assume that the disciples did not doubt Christ's divinity because He healed the sick, raised the dead, and controlled the wind and the waves.

Miracles "Mislead" Knowledge Seekers

Next, Ms. Overall alleges that people are "knowledge seekers" who try to understand the world by "patterns" and "regularities." And since miracles are rare and random compared to ordered natural laws, they "mislead" people by hindering "growth of scientific and philosophical comprehension" of the world. A benevolent God would never do this, she says.

Ignoring for the moment the question of how Ms. Overall could possibly know what God would or would not do apart from what He has told us in Scripture, God has told us that He desires that we see life and the universe as a display of His power, genius, and goodness, and not as self-operating. And even as every natural law displays His glory, every miracle in response to prayer—or as showing His rule over the universe—affirms God's goodness and purposes as revealed in Scripture. Whether they fit a "pattern" is irrelevant—no biblical miracle in its context ever led those who saw them to doubt God's power and existence. Indeed, God desires that all people view the world as His handiwork, and that they likewise see miracles as evidence of His power and generous involvement in the lives of His people. This may not agree with the worldview of atheists, but it certainly displays God's purposes.

Moreover, time and chance produce no laws, "natural" or otherwise. Science and knowledge are impossible apart from God creating and upholding the universe. And while a good God would never mislead His people, He desires that they see the obvious evidence that He created, upholds, and orders it as He pleases. To view the world as operating on its own, and to "scientifically" study it through this lens, contradicts God's revealed purpose in the world:

> Forever, O LORD, Thy word is settled in heaven. Thy faithfulness continues throughout all generations; Thou didst establish the earth, and it stands. They stand this day according to Thine ordinances, for all things are Thy servants. (Psalm 119:89–91)

> Thus says the LORD, your Redeemer, and the one who formed you from the womb, "I, the LORD, am the maker of all things, stretching out the heavens by Myself, and spreading out the earth all alone, causing the omens of boasters to fail, making fools out of diviners, causing wise men to draw back, and turning their knowledge into foolishness." (Isa. 44:24–25)

As Paul told the Athenians, "The God who made the world and all things in it…gives to all life and breath and all things" (Acts 17:24–25). A benevolent God desires in us a humility that views His nature and works correctly.

> "For My hand made all these things, thus all these things came into being," declares the LORD. "But to this one I will look, to him who is humble and contrite of spirit, and who trembles at My word." (Isa. 66:2)

Miracles as "Trivial"

Ms. Overall goes on to say that if God performs miracles, why doesn't He do more to solve the world's problems? An excellent question, and one asked by many believers and unbelievers alike. But again, we can know only what He has chosen to reveal to us, while He has revealed everything we need to trust Him with the affairs of the universe. Yet countless "secret things" lie beyond our limited understanding, thus reminding us that we are not God. And regardless, our limitations do not constitute evidence against His existence.

Ms. Overall describes the miracles of Scripture as "caprice," "bias," and "triviality." She says that because God doesn't cure *everyone*, He doesn't act as someone who is all-powerful, all-knowing, and good. Yet what she calls caprice and bias, Scripture calls God's sovereign and free choice.

Christ tells a parable in which vineyard workers agree with the vineyard's owner to work for a particular rate of pay. At day's end, they're paid that amount—but so are workers who came later and worked far fewer hours. In the climax of the story, the vineyard owner says, "Is it not lawful for me to do what I wish with what is my own? Or is your eye envious because I am generous?" Jesus then concludes, "Thus the last shall be first, and the first last" (Matt. 20:15–16). The parable makes the point that God is free to be generous with what He gives to whomever He pleases.

Does God healing a blind man display caprice because He didn't heal everyone? Does God exerting His rights as the creator and owner of everything constitute injustice? Should we complain when philanthropists give gifts to select recipients? Siblings may cry injustice at unequal gifts around the Christmas tree, but their complaints pose no philosophical or theological threat to God's miracles or existence. God owns all things and owes nothing to anyone. Indeed, every good we enjoy comes by His grace, while every breath we breathe comes by His mercy. His perfect justice will prevail in the end.

Miracles Cannot Display God's Purposes

Ms. Overall argues also that miracles performed in time and space cannot sufficiently display the purposes of a limitless God. Perhaps, but they certainly display His power over life, death, health, the sun in the sky, the properties of reality, and whatever else His miracles involve. As Jesus responded when detractors disputed His right to forgive sins,

> "Which is easier, to say, 'Your sins are forgiven,' or to say, 'Rise, and walk'? But in order that you may know that the Son of Man has authority on earth to forgive sins"—then He said to the paralytic—"Rise, take up your bed, and go home." (Matt. 9:5–6)

Here, as in biblical accounts too numerous to recount here, God's miracles clearly proclaim His purpose and power.

Ms. Overall neglects to cite a single miracle of Scripture, thus failing to show how Christ healing the sick, raising the dead, or calming the storm could prove that God doesn't exist. She fails to show how God's judgments against the gods of Egypt, or His parting of the Red Sea, or His bringing water from a rock could display that God doesn't exist. And she fails to show how the apostles giving legs to the lame and eyes to the blind in Christ's name demonstrate that God doesn't exist. Rather, she imagines what the "Christian God" would or would not do—as opposed to what He did, does, and will do (as revealed in Scripture)—then speculates that biblical miracles fail to meet her imagined criteria. From this she concludes that miracles would give evidence that the "Christian God" does not exist. To again borrow a phrase of Jonathan Edwards, "This is not strong arguing."

To make her case, she would do better to consult Scripture, the written record of the time, place, nature, and purpose of God's miracles on which Christians base their beliefs, including Christ's resurrection from the dead. She would then need to show how they each give evidence that God doesn't exist. Yet she would be hard-pressed to find a single instance that calls into question God's existence and power.

I previously noted difficulties with trusting contemporary reports of miracles as the basis of faith in God. But even with doubt concerning the source of such miracles, no one can deny the possibility of God's existence and ability to perform them, any more than crooks abusing the gospel for money deny the infinite excellence of Christ. In the end, the author merely demonstrates that the biblical worldview doesn't agree with her concept of fairness, her opinions about miracles, and her view of God and the world He created and sustains. But she said nothing to disprove miracles and the God who performs them.

God's Glory in His Miracles

"And the Word became flesh, and dwelt among us, and we beheld His glory, glory as of the only begotten from the Father, full of grace and truth" (John 1:14). That glory, in part, is seen in His miracles, the greatest of which was the resurrection of Jesus, the vindication of His paying the full penalty for our sin that we might have eternal life through faith in Him. Whatever one thinks of contemporary accounts of miracles, the biblical accounts not only provide a proper "scientific and philosophical comprehension" of the world, but point to the source of eternal life and reconciliation with the One who created it.

Chapter Twenty-Six

Multiple Attributes Disproofs: Perfect Creator?

We come to the fourth category of arguments against God's existence presented in *The Impossibility of God*—a "deductive argument based on a contradiction between two or more of God's attributes." The editors present the argument as follows:

1. If God exists, then the attributes of God are consistent with one another.
2. Some attributes of God are not consistent with one another.
3. Therefore, God does not and cannot exist.[1]

In the first essay of this category, Theodore M. Drange presents a survey of ten "incompatible-properties arguments," each following the above argument by presenting a pair of divine "properties" that would be mutually incompatible in God.[2]

Perfection Cannot Create

The first argument claims that God cannot be both perfect and the creator of the universe. "A perfect being can have no needs or wants," while a being that created the universe "must have had some need or want." If God created the universe because He desired to share His love with others, this would constitute a want—and would indicate that God was "incomplete" in some

1. Introduction to "Multiple Attributes Disproofs of the Existence of God," *The Impossibility of God* (Amherst, MA: Prometheus Books, 2003), 181.
2. Theodore M. Drange, "Incompatible-Properties Arguments: A Survey," *The Impossibility of God* (Amherst, MA: Prometheus Books, 2003), 185-197.

way, and thus imperfect.[3]

Scripture of course declares that God is perfect and has no needs or wants. Scripture does *not* teach that God created the world to satisfy a need or to complete something lacking in Himself. We know that God created Eve to "complete" Adam, since God designed mankind to be male and female, each meeting a need in the other. Yet the triune God has never had such a need. The persons of the Godhead have existed eternally in perfect love and communion, without lack and entirely complete.

Why then did God create the universe? As Jonathan Edwards pictures it, God freely chose to make all things from the "overflow of His goodness." Edwards observes that if a fountain tends to overflow, this is no evidence for any "emptiness or deficiency" in the fountain.[4] In short, God made everything because He wanted to—just because. And apart from what He has told us in Scripture, how can anyone know otherwise?

The premise that God had "some need or want" in order to create the universe may reflect the catalyst for many of our own decisions, but what requires projecting this onto God's actions? On what basis can we declare that an infinitely good being cannot share His goodness, and delight in doing so, without meeting a need in Himself? Who can state with authority that a perfect being cannot act according to His nature without impugning it? Again, apart from Scripture, how can anyone know what God can and cannot do?

Scripture tells us that God is perfect, and also tells us what that perfection entails. For one, it says He can do as He pleases, often for reasons we cannot know this side of glory. Other times we're told that He does things for His good pleasure—not from need. Given our fallen nature, we may find it difficult to imagine a benevolent action done with the purest and most selfless of motives, for the mere good of others. But how can we possibly know that God is so constrained? Or that a perfectly good God

3. Drange, "Incompatible-Properties Arguments: A Survey," 186.
4. Jonathan Edwards, "Dissertation Concerning the End for Which God Created the World," in *The Works of Jonathan Edwards*, vol. 8, *Ethical Writings*, ed. Paul Ramsey (New Haven, CT: Yale University Press, 1989), 448.

cannot do something for no other reason than the mere pleasure of it?

Projection and the Grand Presumption

You may have observed that a good many atheistic arguments project our own weaknesses and experience onto God, subjecting Him to the same constraints we face in the material and fallen world. Here, it seems, is a similar projection. Of course, God created us because He delighted to do so, but enjoying His actions in no way requires a need in Him. Scripture describes no such need.

Here again lurks the grand presumption that the author can know, with his limited vantage point and limited human abilities, what an infinite and perfect God can be or do. Yet none can know that an infinite and perfect God cannot create a universe unless He had a need or defect. Consider the following argument:

1. God is perfect and can do whatever He pleases.
2. God created the universe.
3. People who don't know the contents of their neighbor's pantry cannot possibly know why a perfect and infinite God created the universe unless God tells them in Scripture.
4. Therefore, explanations of why God created the universe, apart from what Scripture says, are pure speculation and untrustworthy.

Of course, atheists might object by saying they don't accept Scripture as God's word. But how does that make their speculation—done with their limited vantage point and capabilities—superior to the testimony of Scripture? If the Bible contains no more than the opinions of men and is therefore untrustworthy, so too are the opinions of our modern apostles of atheism. But if Scripture is the word of the God who created and sustains all things, He alone can answer our questions about Himself and ultimate realties.

Chapter Twenty-Seven

Multiple Attributes Disproofs: Immutable and Loving?

Another disproof presented by Drange claims that God cannot be both immutable and all-loving. Since "an immutable being cannot be affected by events," but anyone who's all-loving would have to be "affected by events," therefore God cannot exist. "It is impossible for an immutable being to be all-loving," he concludes. For Drange, "This argument is a particularly forceful one."[1]

Here, as with many of the "multiple attribute" arguments, one or more of the premises suffer from a similar problem. In defining the biblical God out of existence, atheists should be careful to use biblical definitions. Anything can be made impossible, in abstraction, by choosing definitions to that end. For instance, some argue that an immutable God cannot be a personal God, or that He couldn't act in time or know things that change. In the present case, the author defines immutability in such a way that God cannot be affected by events. By that definition, the biblical God cannot exist.

Unchanging Attributes

But does Scripture describe God as unable to respond to events? Apart from Scripture, we all suffer from the same limitations and can only guess about the nature of God beyond that which we know by conscience, creation, and the good things He provides for us. In the present case, Scripture tells us that God is both personal and affected by events. He acts and responds to His people—in time. Yet He remains holy, righteous, omniscient, omnipotent,

1. Theodore M. Drange, "Incompatible-Properties Arguments: A Survey," *The Impossibility of God* (Amherst, MA: Prometheus Books, 2003), 190-191.

omnipresent, perfectly wise, and all-loving. *His attributes do not change.* Thus the biblical definition of God's immutability stands at odds with how Drange defines it. One can easily speculate and define attributes that conflict with other attributes, and Drange has done exactly that.

Mysteries Remain

Of course, this does not deny deep mysteries beyond our grasp. Far from it. I think of the problem of evil, or Christ as both God and man, or God's foreordination and human responsibility for sin. But again, "The secret things belong to God." In the present case, employing the biblical definition of immutability easily answers the argument.

Finally, even if Scripture taught God's changeless nature in a way that we cannot humanly reconcile with other attributes of God, that doesn't make His changelessness untrue. An infinite spirit shares none of the limitations of the universe He created and sustains. If God can be no higher than what we can fully fathom, then most of the arguments in *The Impossibility of God* are sound—but in that case, the person we're arguing about would not be God. In the next chapter, we'll examine an argument where the author seems to admit as much.

Chapter Twenty-Eight

Multiple Attributes Disproofs: Transcendent and Omnipresent?

If God is transcendent, He must exist beyond time and space. But if God is omnipresent, He must exist "everywhere in space," and thus cannot be beyond time and space. Therefore (so the argument goes), God is impossible.

Scripture, however, teaches that God is both beyond all things and present everywhere—at the same time and always. And meeting halfway will not do. Scripture doesn't teach that God is *partially* beyond time and space and *partially* in them. Such a view fails to answer the atheist's claim. Moreover, this "compromise" merely affirms a misplaced faith in human opinion as the final standard of what a transcendent God can be or do. And it debases God.

Whose Definition?

The first problem with the objection involves the author's definition of transcendence. Drange says a transcendent being "cannot exist anywhere in space."[1] According to Scripture, however, God's eternal transcendence does not exclude His existing and acting within the universe He created. Nor does God give up His transcendence by creating and involving Himself within His creation. In a sense, all reality depends on God's presence as He sustains all things by the word of His power (Heb. 1:3). The universe cannot operate on its own. Thus, if the author's definition of transcendence stands, the God of Scripture does not exist. Yet how can Drange know the limits of a transcendent God? Apart from God's

1. Theodore M. Drange, "Incompatible-Properties Arguments: A Survey," *The Impossibility of God* (Amherst, MA: Prometheus Books, 2003), 191.

revelation, he can't.

Beyond Comprehension?

Here again, the atheist's grand presumption is at work, the belief that limited people, by themselves, can know and explain ultimate and spiritual realities. But, as with every claim in *The Impossibility of God*, if Drange can't know the contents of his neighbor's sunroom without a look, how can he define the limits of an infinite spirit?

With respect to God as transcendent and omnipresent, Drange admits this is "something that we are totally unable to comprehend."[2] With this we can agree—to a point. Many truths about God in Scripture are difficult to comprehend. The apostle Peter agrees:

> Therefore, beloved, since you look for these things, be diligent to be found by Him in peace, spotless and blameless, and regard the patience of our Lord to be salvation; just as also our beloved brother Paul, according to the wisdom given him, wrote to you, as also in all his letters, speaking in them of these things, in which are some things hard to understand, which the untaught and unstable distort, as they do also the rest of the Scriptures, to their own destruction. (2 Pet. 3:14–16)

At the same time, the limits of our understanding cannot form the standard of what can be true of God. Drange goes from reasonable in admitting the limits of his knowledge to unreasonable in making definite claims about things he cannot know. At best, he can admit that God doesn't fit what he understands of the universe. Or he can admit that God doesn't fit the definitions employed in his syllogisms. With this we can agree. But to conclude that God cannot exist entails a leap of blind and unwarranted faith. With unjustified speculation we cannot agree.

2. Drange, "Incompatible-Properties Arguments: A Survey," 191.

Chapter Twenty-Nine

Multiple Attributes Disproofs: Justice and Mercy?

Continuing his arguments, Drange targets the belief that God is both an "all-just" and an "all-merciful" judge. Drange asserts that an all-just judge must consistently treat all offenders with exactly the severity they deserve, while an all-merciful judge must treat every offender with less severity than they deserve—and since both cannot be true, therefore God cannot exist.[1]

Interestingly, the Bible presents the exact same problem, and Drange has correctly identified it. In this puzzle we have the fundamental issue facing people under God's righteous condemnation—and we find the basis for the gospel of Jesus Christ. Can God, like a corrupt judge who leaves the guilty unpunished, remain righteous if He ignores the demands of His justice to have mercy on sinners?

The Greatest Commandment

As essential to a proper approach to all difficult theological and philosophical issues, the answer to the vital question above requires understanding the relationship of God to mankind from the start, including our appropriate responsibility to Him as our creator. Once more, God created everything and everyone. From God we have life and every good thing, and apart from Him we have nothing. To Him we owe all things, while He owes us nothing. And as God is infinitely excellent, we should treat Him as His dignity deserves. And so we read, "Hear, O Israel! The LORD is our God, the LORD is one! And you shall love the LORD your God with all your heart and with all your soul and

1. Theodore M. Drange, "Incompatible-Properties Arguments: A Survey," *The Impossibility of God* (Amherst, MA: Prometheus Books, 2003), 191.

with all your might" (Deut. 6:4–5). Christ repeated the mandate as the "greatest" commandment (Matt. 22:37, Mark 12:30, Luke 10:27). Therefore the *Shema* states the *minimum* we owe God as our glorious creator, sustainer, and giver of every blessing.

Sin and Unchanging Justice

Sin, however, fails to treat God as He deserves, either by ignoring what He has told us to do, or by doing what He has told us *not* to do. The penalty for sin includes physical and spiritual death. "The soul who sins will die" (Ezek. 18:4). "For the wages of sin is death" (Rom. 6:23).

We see this first in the garden of Eden:

> And the LORD God commanded the man, saying, "From any tree of the garden you may eat freely; but from the tree of the knowledge of good and evil you shall not eat, for in the day that you eat from it you shall surely die." (Gen. 2:16–17).

When Adam and Eve sinned, they immediately died spiritually when their loving communion with God was shattered and He became their judge and adversary. They hid themselves in shame from the One they once loved and enjoyed. Physical death—that mortal enemy and curse—came later, and has afflicted humanity ever since. "Through one man sin entered into the world, and death through sin" (Rom. 5:12).

Moreover, God's holy dignity and power have not changed, and neither have the nature and requirements of His justice. Scripture presents God as a righteous judge whose strict justice applies to everyone, always, without respect to persons. "Whoever keeps the whole law and yet stumbles in one *point*, he has become guilty of all" (Jam. 2:10). "But the LORD abides forever; He has established His throne for judgment, and He will judge the world in righteousness; He will execute judgment for the peoples with equity" (Psalm 9:7–8). The standard for Adam and Eve applies to everyone. And while Christ fulfilled the Mosaic Law and lived the perfect life of honor and obedience eternally owed to God, the moral duty of all people—as articulated in the Shema and repeated by Christ—remains forever. People owe God perfect love and obedience, always.

Utmost Mercy

At the same time, Scripture teems with descriptions of God's mercy to people of His choosing. For instance:

> What shall we say then? There is no injustice with God, is there? May it never be! For He says to Moses, "I will have mercy on whom I have mercy, and I will have compassion on whom I have compassion." (Rom. 9:14–15)

> He has not dealt with us according to our sins, nor rewarded us according to our iniquities. For as high as the heavens are above the earth, so great is His lovingkindness toward those who fear Him. As far as the east is from the west, so far has He removed our transgressions from us. (Psalm 103:10–12)

Perfect justice and mercy even appear in the same verse: "The LORD, the LORD God, compassionate and gracious, slow to anger, and abounding in lovingkindness and truth; who keeps lovingkindness for thousands, who forgives iniquity, transgression and sin; yet He will by no means leave the guilty unpunished" (Ex. 34:6–7).

Impossible with Men

How can this be? Granted, God is free to do as He wills, when He wills, to whom He wills—and no finite and fallen creature can tell Him otherwise.

> "Will the faultfinder contend with the Almighty? Let him who reproves God answer it." Then Job answered the LORD and said, "Behold, I am insignificant; what can I reply to Thee?" (Job 40:2–4)

Nonetheless, God cannot violate His flawless character, including His perfect justice. Should He pervert justice in a single case, He would cease to be perfect and cease to be God. Moreover, if He applied His strict justice without exception, He could be merciful to none. After all, Adam and Eve were cast out of paradise for *one* sin. So the argument that an all-just and all-merciful God cannot exist would seem to have merit. It would also appear that Scripture has created an unsolvable dilemma, calling into question its own coherence and trustworthiness, as well as the existence of the God it proclaims.

In Christ's encounter with the rich young ruler—who refused to part with his wealth in order to follow Him—Jesus used that man's refusal to illustrate how no one who loves anything more than Christ can enter heaven. When Jesus then said, "It is easier for a camel to go through the eye of a needle, than for a rich man to enter the kingdom of God" (Matt. 19:24), the disciples understood the indictment and asked in astonishment, "Then who can be saved?"

Indeed, "If Thou, LORD, shouldst mark iniquities, O Lord, who could stand?" (Psalm 130:3). "For all have sinned and fall short of the glory of God" (Rom. 3:23). "There is none righteous, not even one" (Rom 3:10). "There is not a righteous man on earth who continually does good and who never sins" (Eccl. 7:20). "Who can say, 'I have cleansed my heart, I am pure from my sin'?" (Prov. 20:9).

All stand guilty before God; all are worthy of His condemnation.

Christ Accomplished Justice and Mercy

From the perspective of the accused, the situation is bleak. God will never relax the demands of His justice to grant mercy—the penalty for sin must be paid. Yet Christ did not leave His disciples in despair. He told them, "With men it is impossible, but not with God; for all things are possible with God" (Mark 10:27; compare Matt. 19:26, Luke 18:27). God Himself would become one of us. God Himself would take our place and satisfy the perfect obedience required by His justice. And God Himself would pay the just penalty we deserve for our disobedience and contempt.

> He had to be made like His brethren in all things, that He might become a merciful and faithful high priest in things pertaining to God, to make propitiation for the sins of the people. (Heb. 2:17)

Long before the earthly ministry of Christ as High Priest, the prophet Isaiah predicted His saving work:

> For He grew up before Him like a tender shoot, and like a root out of parched ground; He has no stately form or majesty that we should look upon Him, nor appearance that we should be attracted to Him. He was despised and forsaken of men, a man of sorrows, and acquainted with grief; and like one from whom men hide their face, He was despised, and we did not esteem Him. Surely our griefs He Himself bore, and our sorrows He carried; yet we ourselves esteemed Him stricken, smitten of God, and afflicted. But He was pierced through for our transgressions, He was crushed for our iniquities; the chastening for our well-being fell upon Him, and by His scourging we are healed. All of us like sheep have gone astray, each of us has turned to his own way; but the LORD has caused the iniquity of us all to fall on Him. (Isa. 53:2–6)

And further:

> By oppression and judgment He was taken away; and as for His generation, who considered that He was cut off out of the land of the living, for the transgression of my people to whom the stroke was due? His grave was assigned with wicked men, yet He was with a rich man in His death, because He had done no violence, nor was there any deceit in His mouth. But the LORD was pleased To crush Him, putting Him to grief; if He would render Himself as a guilt offering, He will see His offspring, He will prolong His days, and the good pleasure of the LORD will prosper in His hand. As a result of the anguish of His soul, He will see it and be satisfied; by His knowledge the Righteous One, My Servant, will justify the many, as He will bear their iniquities. (Isa. 53:8–11)

Indeed, the entire sacrificial system of the Jewish tabernacle and temple foreshadowed God's solution to the dilemma of justice and mercy in saving sinners, including the provision of a priestly mediator between God and mankind (in particular, the high priest who entered the Holy of Holies once a year with the blood of the sacrifice to cover the sins of Israel); the practice of substitution (a lamb for a man); and sacrifice for sin (the death of a substitute in the place of the sinner).

Thus John the Baptist proclaimed upon seeing Jesus, "Behold, the Lamb of God who takes away the sin of the world!" (John 1:29). Christ's perfect obedience met the requirements of God's strict justice in loving God with all His "heart, soul, and might," giving God the Father His due as the supremely excellent creator and sustainer of all. On the cross, He suffered infinite wrath and death in our place, paying the penalty for our sin.

As a man, Christ was the perfect substitute for mankind. As God *and* man, He was the perfect mediator between God and man. And as God, His suffering and death paid an *infinite* penalty for the sin of mankind. This He did once for all time, never to be repeated.

> By this will we have been sanctified through the offering of the body of Jesus Christ once for all. And every priest stands daily ministering and offering time after time the same sacrifices, which can never take away sins; but He, having offered one sacrifice for sins for all time, sat down at the right hand of God, waiting from that time onward until His enemies be made a footstool for His feet. For by one offering He has perfected for all time those who are sanctified. (Heb. 10:10–14)

In His cry from the cross, "It is finished!" (John 19:30), Christ proclaimed the successful accomplishment of God's plan for the ages, the fulfillment of the Old Testament prophecies concerning His redeeming work and the reality of the event foreshadowed in the tabernacle and temple ceremonies—the satisfaction of God's justice for the salvation of souls. The Lamb of God came not to abolish the standard of God's perfect justice, but to satisfy its requirements on behalf of sinners:

> Do not think that I came to abolish the Law or the Prophets; I did not come to abolish, but to fulfill. For truly I say to you, until heaven and earth pass away, not the smallest letter or stroke shall pass away from the Law, until all is accomplished. (Matt. 5:17–18)

Ours by Faith

How then do the benefits of Christ's magnificent work become the possession of the sinner? Through faith in Christ alone.

> For God so loved the world, that He gave His only begotten Son, that whoever believes in Him should not perish, but have eternal life. For God did not send the Son into the world to judge the world, but that the world should be saved through Him. (John 3:16–17)

Our good works can do nothing to earn God's favor; salvation is by grace. Moreover, faith *of itself* cannot satisfy the standard of God's strict justice; Christ alone met the requirement of sinless obedience and payment of the penalty for our disobedience. Saving faith constitutes the open, empty, and unworthy hands that accept the free gift of Christ's satisfaction of God's justice on our behalf. Faith denies any merit of our own to earn acceptance by God as it receives the merit earned for us by Christ.

Moreover, as in marriage the bride and groom are legally united as one in a bond of love, so saving faith unites the believer and Christ in a bond of love. When the bride says "I do" and receives the groom as her husband, all that belongs to him becomes hers. And when the bridegroom says "I do" and receives the bride as his wife, all that belongs to her becomes his. (Granted, most of his junk gets thrown out in the process, but I digress.) In the same way, faith unites to Christ such that the merits of what He accomplished for salvation become the possession of the believer. In a "great exchange," our sins were credited to Christ when He suffered and died on the cross, so that His righteousness in meeting the demands of God's justice on our behalf is credited to us when we embrace Him in faith.

By faith the believer is "covered in the righteousness of Christ":

> He made Him who knew no sin *to be* sin on our behalf, that we might become the righteousness of God in Him. (2 Cor. 5:21).

> For if by the transgression of the one, death reigned through the one, much more those who receive the abundance of grace and of the gift of righteousness will reign in life through the One, Jesus Christ. (Rom. 5:17)
>
> For Christ is the end of the law for righteousness to everyone who believes. (Rom. 10:4)

In this way, salvation by faith upholds God's righteous justice. "Do we then nullify the Law through faith? May it never be! On the contrary, we establish the Law" (Rom. 3:31). The obligation to love the Lord with all our heart, soul, and might remains unchanged as Christ, in perfect righteousness, performed it in our place.

Again, the prophet Isaiah spoke of this:

> I will rejoice greatly in the LORD, my soul will exult in my God; for He has clothed me with garments of salvation, He has wrapped me with a robe of righteousness, as a bridegroom decks himself with a garland, and as a bride adorns herself with her jewels. (Isa. 61:10)

A Small Gate

Sadly, though the "Light of the World" satisfied God's justice and offers forgiveness of sin and eternal life to all who would receive Him as Savior, many reject this precious gift:

> There was the true light which, coming into the world, enlightens every man. He was in the world, and the world was made through Him, and the world did not know Him. He came to His own, and those who were His own did not receive Him. But as many as received Him, to them He gave the right to become children of God, even to those who believe in His name, who were born not of blood, nor of the will of the flesh, nor of the will of man, but of God. (John 1:9–13)

Indeed, "The gate is small, and the way is narrow that leads to life, and few are those who find it" (Matt. 7:14). Why? Here's why:

> And this is the judgment, that the light is come into the world, and men loved the darkness rather than the light; for their deeds were evil. For everyone who does evil hates the light, and does not come to the light, lest his deeds should be exposed. (John 3:19–20)

For the religious deniers of Christ as God and Savior, the principle that our best behavior cannot meet God's standard of justice, or that we cannot by our own merits earn God's favor, will pose a great obstacle to faith in Christ. For atheists and the irreligious, submitting our will to God's sovereign authority is too much to ask—it's "contrary to human dignity," as Kant would have it.

In the end, the battle is fought between two wills: God's will in and through Christ, and our own.

A Persistent Problem

We have in this chapter an example of what besets the best of atheistic arguments. From a human perspective, the justice and mercy of God present an unsolvable problem. But God—who created and sustains all things, who transcends what He made, who determines the rules of reality and defines the nature of justice and mercy—has solved the problem according to *His* wisdom. Yet even if it meets the demands of our human grasp of logic, God's solution appears to many as foolish and unacceptable:

> For the word of the cross is to those who are perishing foolishness, but to us who are being saved it is the power of God. For it is written, 'I will destroy the wisdom of the wise, and the cleverness of the clever I will set aside.' Where is the wise man? Where is the scribe? Where is the debater of this age? Has not God made foolish the wisdom of the world? For since in the wisdom of God the world through its wisdom did not come to know God, God was well-pleased through the foolishness of the message preached to save those who believe. (1 Cor. 1:18–21)

And while God's ways need not be understood fully to be true, nothing that seems unsolvable (from our limited perspective) can constitute a problem in the infinite mind of God. He remains just in having mercy on sinners through faith in Christ, who paid our penalty and satisfied the requirements of divine justice on our behalf. Moreover God is sovereign, answers to no one, and remains under no obligation to have mercy on a single soul, especially those who scorn the person and work of Christ—who suffered infinite wrath from boundless love for the unworthy to purchase for them endless and unmeasurable happiness.

Nothing requires God to have mercy on those who reject Him despite the obvious display of His genius and power in creation, despite the clear evidence of His goodness in every blessing, and despite the knowledge of God in every heart through His law written on the conscience. In each case, God's free choice is neither contrary to His justice or mercy. The penalty for sin will be paid—either vicariously in Christ, or personally without Christ—while His free offer of mercy stands for all who would seek Him.

> For if the word spoken through angels proved unalterable, and every transgression and disobedience received a just recompense, how shall we escape if we neglect so great a salvation? (Heb. 2:2–3)

Chapter Thirty

Single Attribute Disproofs: The Paradox of Omnipotence

We come now to "single attribute disproofs," the last of the five categories of arguments against God's existence in *The Impossibility of God*. One such argument, presented by J. L. Cowan, asserts that if there are things that no being can do, then no being can be omnipotent (that is, able to do anything).[1] And if omnipotence is impossible, then God, who is said to be omnipotent, is impossible. To that end, Cowan cites the well-known riddle of the rock: Can God create a rock so heavy He cannot lift it? If so, then there's something God cannot do—lift the rock. If not, there's also something else He cannot do—make the rock. In either case, God is unable to do something and thus cannot be omnipotent.

Cowan grants that omnipotence cannot be denied because God cannot draw a square circle, since self-contradictory things are "logically vacuous" and "cannot, as a matter of logic, truly be applied to anything."[2] He also grants that omnipotence is not denied if God cannot do "immoral" or "unwise" tasks.[3] Yet Cowan asserts that if he can show two "mutually exclusive" alternatives, each of which are not self-contradictory (a square circle, for example), of which only one of the two could ever be done by God or anyone else, then omnipotence is impossible, and thus God is impossible. The unliftable rock puzzle is one such example. He also uses several earthly analogies to make his case,

1. J. L. Cowan, "The Paradox of Omnipotence," and "The Paradox of Omnipotence Revisited," *The Impossibility of God* (Amherst, MA: Prometheus Books, 2003), 330-336, 337-348.
2. Cowan, 330. Cowan cites Aquinas as having advanced the argument against using "self-contradictory things" as disproving omnipotence. See Thomas Aquinas, *Summa Theologiae*, part I, Q. 25, art. 3.
3. Cowan, "The Paradox of Omnipotence Revisited," 340.

concluding that omnipotence is "as useless in theology as in law or morals or anywhere else."[4]

Context

To begin, a brief survey of God's works will help place the argument in its proper setting. In the beginning, God spoke everything into existence. Moreover, having created reality as we know it, He organizes and upholds every quark, atom, and molecule at every moment, while he directs the trillions and trillions of cells in each human body to do their respective part that we might live, love, and reason. From two cells, each invisible to the naked eye, He formed us in the womb. As for the universe, we have yet to see its edge, and its vastness cannot be measured. Yet He created and upholds it all "by the word of His power" (Heb. 1:2–3).

Moreover, He can change at will the "physical laws" of how He governs all things. He can stop the sun in the sky, create darkness at midday (without an eclipse), raise the dead, heal the sick, give eyes to those born blind, and create a new heaven and new earth. With Baruch we exclaim, "Ah Lord GOD! Behold, Thou hast made the heavens and the earth by Thy great power and by Thine outstretched arm! Nothing is too difficult for Thee" (Jer. 32:17).

Therefore, should no possible solution to the great rock riddle be found, and the riddle's outcome—from our limited perspective—prove supremely authoritative in dictating what transcendent realities can and cannot be, we can at least say that God can speak a universe into existence, including everything in it, even if He can't make or lift that silly rock. Nonetheless, an obvious solution to the riddle exists, while the argument proves to be no more than a word game.

And again, who makes such claims? As we've seen, we share the common weakness of not knowing the contents of our neighbor's playroom without having a look, and we certainly cannot explain exhaustively the nature of an infinite spirit. Sometimes we forget where we put our wallet or purse. We may have taken

4. Cowan, "The Paradox of Omnipotence Revisited," 348.

physics in high school, but can't remember its many theorems. Or we may have a Ph.D. in physics, but have no idea what exists beyond the edge of the universe and the three or four dimensions of our existence. How then can anyone conclude for sure that God cannot exist simply because somebody devised a clever puzzle of logic?

The Solution

Lest I be accused of begging the question with that small bit of context, the argument is no more than semantic sleight of hand. First, God cannot make something so big that He cannot lift it. This is something He cannot do, an impossibility. But rather than indicating a weakness or inability in God, it affirms His omnipotence. The making of the rock and the lifting of it are not mutually exclusive, as Cowan and others would argue. Rather, one is implied by the other. It logically and necessarily follows that a being of infinite power could not make something He couldn't lift.

We can see this clearly if we merely restate the riddle: Can God make a rock of such a weight that no greater weight is possible? Or this: Can God make a rock of infinite weight? The answers are yes and yes. Can God lift such a rock? Yes again. In short, God is omnipotent and can make a rock of infinite weight—and He can lift it.

No doubt this solution will prove unsatisfactory to many. But even if no logical solution can be found to the riddle of the heavy rock, this cannot undo the immeasurable weight of the obvious—the immediately and intuitively known evidence for God's existence. All reality clearly exhibits His genius and power. Moreover, no book could be written or discussion ventured concerning God's existence if He didn't exist. The mere fact that we live and can discuss such things gives definite evidence of God's existence. Reason—let alone the brain, body, and earthly things and systems to support it—would be impossible in a universe founded on random chance. Even "matter" is little more than space (by some accounts, entirely space), with sub-atomic realities held together in a consistent and orderly design, despite properties that would seem to prevent any ongoing and consistent order.

Fancy Bows to Reality

In the end, God created us in His image with the ability to reason, to employ logic to organize our thoughts that we might better know, express, and enjoy His infinite excellence and blessings. That we enlist logic to deny Him may deride His goodness, but it also gives evidence of His existence and our need of a Savior to deliver us from abusing His gifts and insulting His excellence. In any event, God's power and existence are under no more threat from logical puzzles than motion is threatened by the brilliance of Zeno. Abstractions must give way to reality.

Conclusion

When all is said and done, the claims of the atheist reduce to this: "I am God and there is no other." Does this sound extreme? Needlessly pejorative? Or maybe it unfairly links atheism to the heart of sin as displayed in Scripture.

Ever since the rebellion of Lucifer, and that of Adam and Eve, the essence of sin remains the same. Scripture tells us that all sin elevates our will over and against God's will. Every account of God and reality contrary to God's account exalts human opinion over God's revelation. In every sin we assume the place and prerogative of God as sovereign. In every denial of God we elevate our own opinion over God's word as the ultimate source of all truth, knowledge, and how we should live.

The grand presumption of every atheist reads, *I am adequate by myself to know and explain ultimate and spiritual realities.* Consistent with this faith in their own abilities and opinions, they conclude that God cannot be greater than how we experience time, material, space, logic, and knowledge. A God beyond the limits of human understanding is impossible, they say. In other words, nothing can exist that fails to conform to the same "laws" and limits we observe and experience in the world. Despite the inability to know what lies beyond us, they say in effect, "If we cannot grasp or logically reconcile something in our mind, it cannot exist."

Not only do atheists assume they can know what they can't know; they also treat their perspective and opinion as the final measure of what's possible. Claiming science and reason, they embrace irrationality and blind faith.

When all is said and done, atheism does reflect the essence of every sin recorded in Scripture, and every sin written on the tablet of our lives. It says in effect, "I am the final authority. I can do what I want, regardless of what I owe to my Creator, regardless of my need of Him for life and every good thing. I can believe what I want, despite the obvious evidence for His existence, power, genius, and goodness in and around me. I can deny Him, and I can call others to do the same, even though, deep down, I know better."

And—dare I say it—they assert all this despite the fact that they don't know the content of their neighbor's nursery without a look.

In the end, atheists make bold claims they cannot justify. Claiming the high ground of science and reason, they stand on neither. Denying "faith," they embrace irrationality and rely on blind faith in their limited perspectives and opinions about things beyond their purview. They deny the clear revelation of God, even as they ask others to trust the untrustworthy. They reject their Creator and Redeemer as they ask you to place your soul's destiny into the hands of those wholly unqualified to care for it.

True faith and wisdom admit their limits and trust the only One who is worthy of trust. In the person and work of Christ, God has displayed His infinite excellence and unwillingness to compromise His holiness to save a single soul. In infinite love for the unlovable, He saved souls in perfect satisfaction of His unchanging and righteous justice. He fulfilled His promises in a display of infinite excellence, as One worthy to be worshiped, as One to whom we can entrust our soul for eternity. May God produce in us a greater love and faith in His perfect character and promises, and a greater love for those in need of Christ. May He grant us great grace to share truth with love, so that unbelievers might also enjoy God's richest blessings forever, through faith in Christ alone. Amen.

Index

A

F

G

S

Scripture Index